WHAT IS HIP?

THE LIFE AND TIMES OF

THE TRAGICALLY HIP

NY Times Best-seller
MARC SHAPIRO

What is Hip? The Life and Times of The Tragically Hip©
2017 by Marc Shapiro

All Rights Reserved. No part of this book may be reproduced or transmitted in any form or by any means, electronic or mechanical, including photocopying, without permission in writing from the publisher.

For more information contact:
Riverdale Avenue Books
5676 Riverdale Avenue
Riverdale, NY 10471.

www.riverdaleavebooks.com

Design by www.formatting4U.com
Cover by Scott Carpenter

Digital ISBN: 978-1-62601-365-0
Print ISBN: 978-1-62601-366-7

First Edition April, 2017

"When I was in high school and university, we would celebrate [The Tragically Hip] as our local band…at one point we were sure they're going to break out, but you know what, I am so glad they're all ours…Tragically Hip is inexorably part of who and what we are as a country."
  --**Justin Trudeau**, Canadian Prime Minister

"The Tragically Hip is certainly one of the greatest bands we've ever produced in this country."
  - **Geddy Lee** of Rush

THIS BOOK IS DEDICATED TO...

All the people who keep me sane.

Always number one is my wife Nancy. Let me tell you about Nancy. She's beautiful. She's bright, intelligent, and insightful and has a firmer grasp on reality than I can ever hope to have. When I'm bouncing off the walls she brings me back down to earth, with a loving "deal with it" or "the lawn needs mowing." She has never discouraged me but, rather, has been quick with encouragement. We've been together forever. We make the wheels turn in the best possible way. When she needs space, I can sense it. If I can't sense, it she tells me. We've been together forever and we're looking forward to a whole lot more.

Love you Nancy with all my heart.
Marc

TABLE OF CONTENTS

Author's Notes
Enigma Under the Radar

Canadian rock for dummies. Rush, The Guess Who, Bachman-Turner Overdrive, Neil Young, Bryan Adams and Joni Mitchell. And for extra credit there's Gordon Lightfoot who is not really rock, but he is most definitely Canadian. If you think you aced this quiz…well, I'll give you a generous B. An A would have required you to dig a bit deeper. It would have required you to be hip to The Tragically Hip.

"The Tragically who?" That's what I figured. Just a band that only a small fraction of the planet even knew existed despite the fact that the band has the distinction for having opened for both The Rolling Stones and Led Zeppelin. But as I did the requisite research and made my attempts at tracking down those who knew the band, I discovered a salient bottom line. The Tragically Hip were a decent bunch of guys, good to fans and family to a fault, made heartfelt and thoughtful music and have ultimately been loyal to their Canadian roots. They are rock musicians, so nobody is ever going to mention them in the same breath as boy scouts and choirboys. But what I discovered as I dug deep into the life and history of the band was that they were awfully damned close.

Marc Shapiro

The Tragically Hip (Gord Downie, Rob Baker, Gord Sinclair, Paul Langlois and Johnny Faye) are an enigma on a grand scale. Together more than 30 years (without a lineup change unless you count the sax player who split very early on). Few, if any, had ever heard of them outside of their native Canada and those who have only know them by way of Canadian rock stations whose signals have managed to leak across to the US's Pacific Northwest or the occasional live foray across the border. But The Tragically Hip's seemingly manic determination to stay close to home has definitely had an upside.

Their musical output, to date, includes 14 studio albums, two live albums, one EP, 54 singles, nine of which have reached #1 on Canadian charts and 14 Juno awards (Canada's Grammys). The Tragically Hip are Canada's equivalent of Bob Dylan and Led Zeppelin rolled into one. At last count, the band reportedly has approximately 11 million Internet followers, who, to a degree buy into a tribal, Grateful Dead vibe, the presence of which has regularly resulted in sold-out concerts and club dates since 1983.

Musically the band's bread and butter has been described as an often ethereal, introspective mixture of rock, blues and country. A lot of critics have been quick to describe what The Tragically Hip do as "alt this" or "alt that." What is known for a fact is that the band has always been a bunch of good old fashioned team players; each member taking a swing during a song, often so subtle or low key as to inspire questions of what audiences had actually heard, en route to a group interpretation of their material.

This is a lot of music cred from a band which has

2

maintained such a low key personal and professional profile that, if you're in Toronto while you're reading this, the chances are good that you just passed members of the band on the street without batting an eye. Consequently, there are endless questions to be asked and answered.

Such as...

Why has there not been a biography of The Tragically Hip before and why, all of a sudden, is there this book now? I don't know why there has never been another book on The Tragically Hip. Loyalty to the band's privacy? A lack of pop culture hipness on the part of the publishing industry? How can anyone write a book about a band a large percentage of the world does not even know exists? The hows and whys surrounding the lack of a Tragically Hip book until now are endless.

As to the why now?

The band recently announced that their lead singer, Gord Downie, has brain cancer and, as of this book, his and the band's future are clouded by uncertainty. So, in the all business lexicon of the world of the pop culture/celebrity publishing industry, what better time to cash in?

Let's get the obvious out of the way before you start throwing the brickbats and Internet invective. I'm not overly fond of doing books that have even the perception of a 'death watch' attached to them. But I have done them.

My book on George Harrison, *Behind Sad Eyes: The Life and Career of George Harrison*, was actually written well in advance of The Beatles' guitarist's passing but with the knowledge that he was not in the best of health. It was only due to the proclivities of book publishing that the book came out shortly after Harrison's actual death and I took some heat for that. Less than eight hours after the plane carrying singer Jenni Rivera crashed into a Mexican mountain range, I had a deal in place to write the story of her life and subsequent passing. Also took some heat for that one. Not so much heat for that one but guilty as charged. And finally there was that marathon of my Annette Funicello book that was commissioned, at least initially, to coincide with her death. The book sat with the original publisher for eight years before everybody's favorite Mousketeer passed.

But before you get out the tar and feathers, there was one thing that drove me to do all three of those books. Each person I chronicled had an amazing life worth writing about. That I was writing the book either at or near the end of their respective lives was admittedly part calculating and part homage.

Which leads me to the reason de jour why I wanted to write *What Is Hip? The Life and Times of the Tragically Hip*. Quite simply I wanted the whole story of a group that is considered a ghost to many but that ultimately has had a living, breathing story to tell.

As always, research was an overriding challenge. Canadian media was quick to pick up on the Hip, literally covering them from their inception on to the present. US and most international press? Not so much. Getting people to talk on the record about the band was a crapshoot. Some talked. One or two danced around it. Some ignored my interview requests and one said he would send me some pertinent information on the condition that his name not appear anywhere in the book. Needless to say, the information was good and his name is nowhere to be found. Others bluntly refused to be involved. In a matter of hours, another went from enthusiastically saying they were all in to "I don't feel comfortable doing this."

Let's get one thing straight. The Tragically Hip is not the kind of band that lends itself to scandal. I was not looking for it. But if it was there and it could be verified...Well you get the picture. At the end of the day, a few things were hinted at but could not be verified and so, in the name of real journalism, I did not use it. Which is part and parcel of the way this book came together. Solid research and nothing more. Which is usually the way most good stories go.

As you are reading this, the story of The Tragically Hip may finally have come to an end. I'm a big believer in karma and I've never shunned away from the idea of miracles. I do know that, as this book goes to press, The Tragically Hip were making tentative plans. But one thing was certain.

The Tragically Hip had just finished a tour and now they were going fishing.

Marc Shapiro 2016

Introduction
Just Tell Me the Truth

The Tragically Hip lead singer Gord Downie was, reportedly, walking on a cloud as he meandered down the street in his hometown of Kingston, Ontario in November 2015. And with good reason.

The band had recently concluded the sessions for their latest album, entitled *Man, Machine, Poem* and word of mouth was that The Tragically Hip, 30 plus years on, had taken a giant step forward creatively. Those privy to the sessions, and the final results, were effusive in their praise of how the album straddled a perfect line between familiar, esoteric and challenging, and had taken a daring approach to tackling subject matter both subtle and in-your-face. There was even talk that *Man, Machine, Poem* might well be the album to finally kick open the door to major US acceptance.

Consequently Downie's thoughts were in a good place as he walked down the familiar streets of his youth. The first single would be out in April and the band would kick off a month long tour of Canada shortly after that. Christmas was coming early to Downie and he couldn't be happier. Suddenly, as reported by *CBC News* and countless other media outlets, Downie collapsed onto the street…

…in the throes of a massive seizure.

The singer was rushed to a nearby hospital emergency room and was immediately given a battery of tests. The results were surprising and not good.

Dr. James Perry, an Oncologist who heads up the Neurology Department of Canada's Sunnybrook Health Sciences Center and who is an admitted, lifelong Tragically Hip fan, was used to receiving referral emails from other surgeons. These emails usually were, in a medical sense, a cry for help or instruction on what to do and how to proceed. It was rarely good news but as Dr. Perry would recall in a *CBC Music* article, this referral struck particularly hard. The name on the referral was Gord Downie and the email on the referral was for a particularly aggressive form of brain cancer called glioblastoma.

"I emailed back," recalled Perry. 'Is this a coincidence or do you really mean 'that' Gord Downie?' The referring surgeon wrote back 'No I really mean…"

Perry's shock and sadness were based on his knowledge of the disease. Glioblastoma is a particularly virulent cancer strain, treatable to a degree but ultimately inoperable and finally fatal. And it is a disease that has taken the lives of the famous. Among the noted personalities who were succumbed to glioblastoma were US Senator Ted Kennedy, professional baseball player Gary Carter, legendary singer and actress Ethel Merman, composer George Gershwin, the inventor of the modern synthesizer Robert Moog and, most recently, Beau Biden, son of the US Vice President Joe Biden.

Downie's reaction to the news, not surprisingly, came in waves of shock, surprise, no small amount of depression but, ultimately, a dogged determination to keep a positive attitude and to do whatever had to be done. This was not the first time the Downie family had fought cancer. His wife, Laura Leigh Usher, had fought cancer and won the battle a few years previously and, in a 2012 interview with *CBC's* George Stroumboulopoulos, Downie revealed the turmoil in his wife's situation that, doubtless, was in him now as well.

"There were a lot of emotions," he related. "You know, anger, fear, impatience. Impatience is the big one. Love. You're just clamoring for help."

Dr. Douglas James Cook, a neurosurgeon at Kingston General Hospital where Downie's treatment would take place, had a front row seat to how Downie, emotionally, was handling what was truly a life and death situation. He reported to *The Kingston Whig Standard* that "He's been nothing but courageous through the whole thing. He's got a very strong family. They're a very strong group, very supportive. He's very loved."

But true to his very private nature, Downie was cautious. His family and bandmates were the first to know and that was it for a time. But there was the upcoming record release to consider and, perhaps more taxing, the tour that was already sold out in most venues. However, Downie was a first things first kind of guy. Which meant treating the cancer.

The first step was a late November preliminary surgery to gather tissue samples for the purpose of diagnosis and a plan of treatment. Shortly thereafter, Cook had the singer on the operating table once again for a marathon surgery to remove the tumor. The neurosurgeon described the details of the surgery with *The Kingston Whig Standard.*

"He went through a five-hour, awake brain surgery where we mapped out his speech areas and removed a portion of his temporal lobe which was where the tumor was."

The result was a successful and promising procedure but, as Cook explained, the result was also mixed. "Gord's singing and speech were not affected by the surgery. But the cells causing the cancer are still active and can't be cured."

While Downie continued to recover from the surgery, there was a lot of soul searching within his family and within the band. Downie and the rest of the band remained cautiously optimistic about the new album and, even more cautiously, about the proposed tour. In their hearts, the band knew that word of Downie's illness would inevitably leak out and that their legions of fans would be devastated. But there would be time to deal with those issues later. Right now, the most important thing was that Downie get the best possible treatment available.

By mid-March, Downie was on a comprehensive, five day a week treatment program that involved a combination of radiation treatment coupled with oral chemotherapy drugs. The end of April indicated that there was some positive news. Dr. Cook told *The Globe and Mail* that the type of cancer Downie had was known to respond well to treatment and that the prognosis was good for a longer period of survival. However Cook cautioned that "Glioblastoma is amongst the deadliest tumors that we get. It is one that we don't have a cure for."

For The Tragically Hip, the dire prediction was more than balanced out by the doctor's insistence that, under certain monitored treatments and monitoring, there was no reason why Downie could not sing and perform live.

That was all Downie and the rest of the band needed to hear.

The band immediately went into secretive rehearsals in an attempt to determine if Downie, post treatment, would be up to the rigors of live performing. On hand for several of those rehearsals was Dr. Perry to monitor Downie during the rehearsals. Dr. Perry would later concede that being a life-long Tragically Hip fan meant more than a doctor/patient exercise. "He's doing very well," he would state. "They've started rehearsing and I was lucky enough to see a few of those rehearsals. They were very good."

By May, Downie had been given the official okay to tour. That moment also signaled the time when The Tragically Hip would finally have to go public with the news of Downie's cancer. Despite their best efforts, there had been rumbles along the Internet and fan pages that something might not be right in The Tragically Hip universe. On May 19, the band members were honored at Queens University (the college they attended but never graduated from) with honorary degrees. But all the inspiring words from the band to graduating students could not dissuade the media from the most compelling story. And that was that Downie was not there.

A May 24 press conference was scheduled to lay it all out to the band's legion of fans. But, ever loyal to the fans, the band decided that it would be more appropriate to break the news in a more personal way.

And so, hours before the planned press conference, the band posted a story on The Tragically Hip website. It read in part, "Hello friends. We have some very tough news to share with you today and we wish it wasn't so." The website message went on to disclose the nature of Downie's cancer and explained that the band's singer had had surgery and post- surgery treatment and had been cleared to go on a planned tour in support of their new album.

The press conference took place at the Sunnybrook Health Sciences Center amid a cloud of rumor and speculation. There had been a sense that something was wrong all along amongst The Tragically Hip fan community and, with the band's website announcement, there was a sense of sadness, disbelief and heartbreak that quickly spread across Canada. The only thing that the press conference, which was attended by many Canadian and US media outlets including *Billboard*, could do was set the record straight.

The band, having made it official earlier in the day, did not attend. Which left the role of messenger bearing bad tidings to Dr. Perry. "It is my difficult duty to tell you that Gord Downie's tumor is incurable," he told the assembled press. "But [post treatment] MRI's shows substantially less brain swelling and only a residual amount of tumor was visible." Perry further acknowledged that, given those results, he felt secure in okaying the band to go on tour."

The press conference continued in a celebratory vibe with the band's co-manager Patrick Shamrock stoking the expectation of The Tragically Hip's new music and the tour of Canada to begin July 22. "This [music] is what the guy's do, so when this started to happen the tour was certainly a goal. The band had a new record that they were really proud of and knowing Gord, he was like 'I want to play these songs for people.'"

In the wake of the press conference, the media was alive with speculation, much of it medical in nature, on the now most famous cancer patient on the planet. Questions about how long a person with this kind of brain tumor could expect to live were asked and answered by Dr.'s Perry and Cook who had suddenly become the most sought-after interviewees in music journalism. People wanted to know what symptoms to look for if, heaven forbid, Downie's condition took a turn for the worse. Glioblastoma was very much a trending topic on the Internet. In a way it was all kind of morbid.

Buy ultimately it was the band's quiet confidence and immense loyalty to the people who had gotten them to this point in their career and life that many, through their most fervent hopes and dreams for the band, could not help but slip into melancholy with the idea that this might, truly, be the last hurrah.

"We're going to dig deep," they related in their website message. "We're going to try and make this our best tour ever."

Chapter One
Growing Up in Prison Town

Kingston is one of those towns that has always seemed to have everything going for it. Nestled in Eastern Ontario, at the eastern end of Lake Ontario, the town, whose population hovers regularly around the 120,000 range, is known for a lot of things.

Kingston's sense of history and respect for architecture resulted in it regularly being referred to as "the Limestone City." It annually shows up as one of the best places to live and work in Canada. The town has an active culture and arts community that has been a constant tourist draw. And with tongue firmly planted in cheek, Kingston, in informal conversation, is often referred to as Prison Town because of the seven correctional institutions (down from nine because of recent closures) that are located in Kingston.

But as The Tragically Hip once proclaimed in a *Queen's University Journal* story, the magic of the town is ultimately in its people. "Kingston is an odd town. It's made up of quasi-disparate groups. You've got the townies and the university kids, the college kids and the people from the east end and the people from the west end who all live together under this spectrum of amalgamation and a sense of community."

Kingston was definitely the kind of town people flocked to, especially in the late 50's and early 60's when the town had remained largely undiscovered and the real estate prices were comparatively reasonable. Especially to the likes of Edgar and Lorna Downie.

Originally from Belfast, Northern Ireland, the Downies and their three children saw greener pastures across the Atlantic and made their way to Oakville, Ontario. Edgar could, reportedly, sell ice to Eskimos and almost immediately found work as a travelling salesman; selling everything from cutlery and flatware to women's underwear on a route through Ontario and Quebec. Edgar was on the road a lot and so it fell to Lorna to raise the couple's brood of three children. On the occasion of Lorna announcing that she was now pregnant with the couple's fourth child, Edgar made the decision that it was time to come off the road and settle into a sales job that would require less travel

The couple moved to Amherstview, a small town on the northern end of Lake Ontario and a stone's throw from Kingston. Amherstview was another town in the midst of a growth spurt and Edgar took the opportunity to get his real estate license and made a solid living selling houses to fellow newcomers. Not long after Edgar sold his first property, Lorna went into labor.

Gordon Edgar "Gord" Downie was born February 6, 1964. A good birthday for rock stars, as Bob Marley, Axl Rose (Guns and Roses) and Rick Astley also shared Downie's birthdate.

Downie grew up in a loving, family-oriented and

outdoors-inclined environment where, not surprisingly, sports and, particularly, hockey were pivotal elements of his childhood world. He was instantly drawn to the rural nature of Amherstview but, in later years, and with the inherent tag of nearby Kingston so attached to his name, would concede that not actually being born in Kingston had always stayed with him. "I came from a rural area," he remarked in the book *Have Not Been the Same: The CanRock Renaissance*. "I wouldn't say that it has given me a stigma but it's something that's on my mind."

Although the family was much more settled and Edgar rarely traveled, Downie recalled in a *Toro Magazine* interview that family trips were times he relished. "Our family road trips still loom as epochal events in my life. There must be something about seeing new things with the people you love."

Downie was quick to take his cues from his older siblings at a very early age and, almost from the time he could walk, he would be following his, at the time, two older brothers and a sister, on playtime along the rocky shoreline of Lake Ontario.

"I fished all the time as a kid in Lake Ontario," he reminisced in a conversation with *Maclean's*. "But I never caught a big fish, ever. As a kid we spent every waking moment up and down the rocky shore. We used to tie a shipping rope to a pitchfork and try to spear big carp. But we never got one."

Not surprisingly, professional hockey was very much at the center of Downie's psychological profile growing up in Amherstview. The family would, almost daily, live and die by the games of their beloved Bruins. And it was the quite athletic Downie who gravitated toward the youth hockey leagues by the time he was six. The Emestown Raceway Auto Parts Bantams, with Downie in goal much of the time, were the reigning local sports story during the decade of the 70's and would go to the Provincial Championship Round in 1979.

Never one to take anything at face value, Downie, in conversation with *TSN,* acknowledged a near existential approach to playing in the net. "I liked the independence of playing goalie. It was almost like I was playing a different game."

Downie, in conversation with *Maclean's,* saw much more in the sport than just a good time for kids. "The crowds at those games were huge. The stakes were brutal and crushing. It teaches you things."

One of the things it taught him was that he was quite good at the sport. So much so that, in his pre-teen years, Downie was approached by the Kingston AA Rep Team to join them. In Kingston circles, the AA Rep Team was considered an important first step on the road to professional stardom in the sport and Downie had to admit that he was considering the offer. That is until his father stepped in and said no. Joining the team would have meant regular, long distance travel and parental duty as chaperones. Edgar indicated, in *TSN,* that he was too busy selling houses locally and making a living to go on the road for kids' youth hockey.

Downie's character was being molded on many different levels. He was quite capable of turning from a fun-loving extrovert to a quiet introvert at a moment's notice. For those privy to the young boy's turns, it was always an entertaining prospect. One person who had a front row seat on Downie's chameleon-like personality was childhood friend Martina Fitzgerald who recalled to *CBC News* that Downie "was funny, athletic and kind without trying to be the center of attention."

As Downie entered his pre-teen years, it was discovered that he could also be quite spontaneous. So much so that, as he explained in *Toro*, sometimes what he did would even surprise him. Witness the day he danced in public for the first time. "The first time I danced, it was the Grade 7 dance at the school gym. I remember the song being fast. I went for it and loved it. A dancer has no peers. Only partners."

Not long after he tried his dancing skills out in public for the first time, he matriculated to Emestown Secondary School for his first two years of middle school. His years at Emestown would see change. While he still maintained an undying fervor for the Bruins hockey team, his overall interest in sports was fading away in deference to two other normal teenage pursuits...

...Girls and music.

Phil Baker had the makings of a top-flight legal professional in 1947. He was whip smart, a real student of the law and, according to anybody who met him, he had a substantial sense of humor. That same year, Baker would find his soulmate in a like-minded quasi ex-patriot named Mary. The woman who would become Mary Baker had established quite the athletic reputation while growing up just this side of the Ontario/United States border. The year they met, Mary had just captured the prestigious United States Figure Skating Dance Championship. She was attractive, intelligent and mentally quick on her feet, easy going in just about any situation. Paul and Mary met at a Toronto Skating Club and, immediately, became a love match. Their relationship blossomed in a casual, steady pace before they finally married in 1952.

The Bakers moved to the Churchill Crescent district of Kingston. Long considered upper class and a hotbed of liberal social and political values, the Baker family expanded along with Baker's career that eventually saw him rising to the level of district court judge in Kingston. Rob, the couple's third child (following Mathew and Vicki) was born April 12, 1962.

The Baker children were brought up amid fairly traditional values but, perhaps guided by Mary's more theatrical and creative background, were fairly liberal when it came to the creative arts and all three children were encouraged to indulge in creative especially when it came to music. And in the case of Rob, music was love at first sight.

Initially, it was monkey see-monkey do. Mathew had taken to the guitar at a fairly young age and the even younger Rob decided he wanted to follow suit. Baker started out his musical career by playing air guitar as he related in a *Kickass Canadians.com* interview. "I'd get so into the music. I'd pretend that I was playing all the instruments with all my body parts. I'd just become a giant, quivering spastic mess on the floor."

Baker would soon graduate to a different level of make believe as he revealed in a *Reverend Guitars.com* interview that his axe of choice had evolved from invisible to a tennis racket. "I was leaping off the furniture pretending to play along to songs by David Bowie and Led Zeppelin with a tennis racket. I'd get so into the music."

Baker's infatuation had actually transformed into downright obsession by the time he turned 12 and had begun picking out simple chords on his brother's guitar. "I was always really impressed by people who could whip out a guitar and having a group of people silently hanging on every word or note. I secretly harbored a desire to be able to do that," he told *Reverend Guitars.com.*

Baker's father was quick to notice his son's interest in music and the guitar and, on the occasion of his 13th birthday, presented Baker with an early 70's model Stratocaster. That proved to be the final push into the great unknown of guitars and rock. Baker soon began networking with other novice rock stars in the neighborhood and would spend all his free time practicing and jamming in any spare room he could find.

Among the most available was the basement of Baker's childhood friend and budding musician in his own rite, Gord Sinclair. Sinclair, born in 1962 to Dean (Dean of Medicine at Queens University) and Leona Sinclair, always had music in his life. From an early age, there was music in the Sinclair house all the time, courtesy of Gord's parents' penchant for big band music. As he grew, Sinclair did not need much encouragement to expand his own musical horizons. Early on, he gravitated toward the bagpipes and made a big impression while playing in the Rob Roy Pipe Band. Later he would pick up the fife as a featured player in the Fort Henry Guard. Much later, he would dabble with the piano before developing a true passion for all string instruments.

Which meant that Sinclair, who had known Baker since the pair turned three years old, literally living right down the street, was now spending even more time with Rob. Their musical instincts tended to mesh, with lots of blues-rock and an emphasis on 70's groups like The Yardbirds and Them. With Sinclair's parents more than willing to offer up their basement for practice sessions, Baker and Sinclair would spend hours together, attempting to master the heavy hits of the day. Both were quite good on guitar, but Sinclair recalled in *Canoe.com* that by the time they entered high school things, musically, were getting serious and that meant that one of them would have to blink.

"I first started playing bass with Robby in high school," he recalled. "It was 'friend puts rock band together, younger friend wants to join the band but can't play guitar, plays bass.' That's how it all started."

How it all started for guitarist Paul Langlois is pretty much open to speculation. After considerable amounts of research, it is a safe bet that no detailed biography really exists. Which is not surprising when you realize that Langlois has always been a pretty much below the radar kind of guy. So we go with what we have.

Paul Langlois was born on August 23, 1964 in Ottawa, Ontario according to a notation in *Prezi.com*. His father Adrien was a high school teacher. Outside of the fact that he was a rabid hockey fan while growing up, and some indications that the young boy was creatively inclined, there are few clues to indicate future musical greatness. Except for a conversation with *The Whig.com* with Langlois' mother Terry in which she indicated that the seeds were definitely planted.

"Certainly I saw music as Paul's lifeblood and he did too," she recalled. "It really came late when he started playing the guitar. But it was his thing to do. He was doing it all of the time. I knew it was going to be his life."

Langlois continued to play it low key. He reportedly jammed with fellow musicians but, allegedly, never performed in a concert or club setting.

There would be more in the Langlois odyssey.

It would be some years before drummer Johnny Fay came within sniffing distance of The Tragically Hip. But fairly early on, it became evident that Fay, born August 30, 1966, had music in his soul.

"I used to hang out with these two brothers in Kingston and they got me into bands like Yes and Rush and all kinds of live music," Fay recalled in a *Canadian Musician* interview. "Along the way, I started getting into drummers like Neil Peart, Alan White, Andy Newmark and Mickey Curry."

But it would be one particular drummer who would turn Fay toward a life in music. "I started playing drums because of Stewart Copeland," Fay revealed to *The Globe & Mail*. "A friend of mine gave me a Police bootleg from Australia when I was in public school. I played it over and over and wore it out. Stewart Copeland was the reason I play drums."

Fay's parents encouraged his interest. But they came from a tradition bound work ethic that meant that, when it came to buying the tools of the trade, Fay was on his own. "My parents were supportive but they didn't buy me anything," he told *Canadian Musician*. "I would always ask for things like a hi hat or a bass drum pedal and, even at Christmas, I would never get it. Their attitude was that if I wanted something bad enough, I had to work for it and so I spent a lot of time working as a bus boy. That was a good thing. I remember buying a hi hat and a snare drum one summer and it just gave me a sense of 'wow!' Then I ran out of money and I would use my mother's knitting needles because she wouldn't give me money to buy new drum sticks."

Fay would work his way through public and middle school, growing in his confidence and skills; all the while learning an important lesson from his parents about the correlation between talent and drive. "I didn't have a ton of talent but I had a lot of drive," he related to *Canadian Musician*. "I knew that if I stuck to something, I was going to get where I wanted to be."

Chapter Two
Before They Were Hip

Baker and Sinclair had seemingly spent years in each other's basement and in rehearsal halls, learning rock licks and imagining the possibilities music had to offer. But by the time they entered Kingston Collegiate and Vocational high school in 1980, they knew that, musically, it was time to walk the walk.

Kingston Collegiate had been around forever, was bound in tradition, yet encouraging to individual thinkers. One of the school's teachers, Hank Connell, recalled in a *Maclean's* piece that the future members of The Tragically Hip, who he had in both his health and science and physical education classes, were typical teenagers. "All the boys were in my Grade 10 science class. I enjoyed having those boys around because they knew when to be quiet and when to be involved in a floor hockey game."

Students seemed to instinctively gravitate toward like minds, so it was not surprising that Baker and Sinclair soon made the acquaintance of fellow students seriously into music. It was at that point that Baker and Sinclair made the jump to performing in their very first band…

Rick and the Rodents. Or to those who considered themselves hip at the time, The Rodents.

According to obscure website information, The Rodents (which also included John Estabrooke, Andrew Grenville and Richard McCreary) formed in 1977 on the KCVI campus for the sole purpose of playing campus variety shows and the occasional dance. They played a solid series of covers of Stones, Kinks, Clash and Jam, among others, and apparently brought the house down. The Rodents would continue their sporadic campus appearances until 1981 when the band dissolved in the name of higher education.

But for their time, Rick and the Rodents were the hottest band on campus. One of those who was an eyewitness to their popularity was a recent transfer to Kingston Collegiate named Gord Downie who waxed nostalgic on The Rodents' stardom in the book *Have Not Been the Same: The CanRock Renaissance*. "The Rodents were kind of a punk band and they were very revered. Rob would walk the halls and people definitely knew who he was. It was an amazing thing."

As it would turn out, Downie was in the midst of a musical life conundrum all his own. His affinity for music and, particularly, 70's style rock had become a constant in his life about the time his mania for sports, primarily hockey, had begun to slip away. But Downie, like most teens, did not seem to have a clue as to what would come next.

"I was never a guy hell-bent on success," he admitted in an *Ottawa Citizen* interview excerpt. "I assumed I would just fall into some sort of job at some point and that would be it."

But during his first year at Kingston Collegiate,

music always seemed to be lingering in the shadows. He became friends with other musicians, in particular Baker and Sinclair. And while Downie, in his fantasies, saw himself as a rock star, he never had the inclination to pick up an instrument. In his mind, Downie saw himself as a frenetic, near spastic front man. The reality was that nobody had seen the youngster sing. Even Downie had moments of doubt. But he was nothing if not brave and so when another high school combo called The Slinks made it known along the grapevine that they were looking for a singer, Downie did not think twice about approaching the band for an audition.

Nobody seems to remember how Downie's audition for The Slinks was received. But the result was that Downie convinced the band that he could sing and walked away with the job. "I felt like the guy who just weaseled his way into some band with the attitude of 'I don't know how to sing but I like to sing,'" he said in the *Ottawa Citizen*.

The Slinks were cut from the same pedigree as The Rodents, a cover band hoping to live out the high school dream of playing at Kingston Collegiate talent shows and after school dances. During their short existence, the band was constantly in a state of transition. From Teenage Head covers to bluesy versions of the Stones, Doors and Junior Wells and the occasional and daring for their time covers of David Bowie and Iggy & The Stooges songs, the band survived on a very miniscule scale, thanks, to a large extent, to the addition of Downie who, even in his Slinks' days, was considered a dynamo on stage; plaintive vocals coupled with a frantic, often demented stage presence. Joe Pater, a former classmate and, for a time, a member of The Slinks, recalled in a blog "doing the blues songs worked real well with the way Gord sang."

The Slinks gigs were comparable to what The Rodents were doing at the time; KCVI talent shows and school dances. But The Slinks managed a handful of gigs off-campus with talent show appearances at places like The Yacht Club, The Polish Hall and what Pater described as "an outdoor show on a farm." Eventually The Slinks came a cropper, due largely to a clash of egos allegedly centered around Downie quickly emerging as the center piece of the band and the first pangs of creative differences with Downie reportedly wanting to incorporate original material into the band's all covers set. History would show that The Slinks, minus Downie and Pater, would last for a few more shows before calling it a day.

The author contacted Pater via email in an attempt to fill in the gaps on his time with Downie and The Slinks but he insisted that his blog memories were all he had to add except for one thing. "The thing I would like to emphasize is how hard Gord worked to become the musician he became."

During their day, The Slinks were considered the next best things to Rick and the Rodents, which inevitably bred some competition between the two groups. Through their mutual interest in music, Downie, Baker and Sinclair would become what Baker described in a *Whig Standard* conversation as "More acquaintance friends than real friends."

But Downie, who like musical competitors Baker and Sinclair, was by this time coming to the end of their high school years, would not be out of work too long. Finny McConnell, a self-described bad boy, was also coming to the end of his association with yet another high school band, Pressure Drop. McConnell had a yen to go to England to soak up the musical vibe but was lacking the finances to get him there. McConnell's father had a suggestion. Downie's talents had begun to seep out into Kingston proper and the elder McConnell suggested to his son that, if he could get Downie to team up with him in yet another band, dubbed The Filters, he would give them a house band gig in his bar for a week, which would more than cover McConnell's trip to the UK.

McConnell did not need too much convincing when his father suggested Downie for The Filters. Years later, he would regale both *The Whig Standard* and *The North Bay Nugget* with just how good he thought the young singer was. "From the moment I saw him play at the KCVI gym [as part of The Slinks], I thought 'Ok, this guy is going to be a rock star.' He had the moves like Iggy Pop and the swagger of Mick Jagger. Let's face it, Gord was a great front man even at that age."

The week-long gig at McConnell's father's bar was successful. Reportedly The Filters were rough and raw and enticing in their punked up covers of classic rock songs, with fun being the operative word when it came to Downie's vocals and stage antics. His spastic gyrations and exaggerated rock star swagger and shouting vocals were the perfect elixir for the alcohol-fueled crowds. The week-long gig made the requisite amount of money, which allowed McConnell to finance his trip to England and, affectively, broke up The Filters.

27

Downie returned to the fairly mundane life of Kingston. His two music buddies, Baker and Sinclair, had put their heyday in The Rodents aside and had matriculated to Queen's University two years earlier. The pair had made overtures toward a non-musical life and were reportedly diligent in their studies (Baker majoring in Visual Arts and Sinclair in History), but could not completely shake music from their souls. The trio would continue to jam and rehearse informally with other musicians but, for the most part, had gone their separate ways. For his part, Downie, who reportedly majored in film for reasons he, to this day, could not remember, basically sleepwalked through his college days, getting by in many instances on borrowed notes and just enough actual appearances in class to keep instructors guessing. Inevitably, Downie, Baker and Sinclair reunited and began to play.

A couple of years behind, Fay had just entered grade 11 in Kingston Collegiate. He was constantly playing drums but had reportedly never showcased his talents in public. Still undecided on what to do next, Fay had stumbled into the world of journalism and, more as an afterthought than anything else, had decided that he would go to Carleton University and get a degree in Journalism. At that point, Fay would often admit that music was more of a hobby than anything else. But it was a hobby that seemed to be taking over his reality.

As for Paul Langlois, well he was pretty much a mystery man at that point. His past has always been pretty much vague at best. If there were any musical adventures prior to The Tragically Hip, they're still pretty much a mystery.

While they had never played in a band together, the trio found something enticing and welcoming in the way they played. Music became an extension of their friendship and their mutual respect for each other and their talents. While the thought of creating their own band may well have crossed their minds, there seemed to be no rush to take that next step...

Until Finny McConnell re-entered the picture. His sojourn to the UK had been fun and, by degrees, enlightening. But soon reality and a lack of funds forced McConnell to return to Kingston, where he decided the best way to turn a buck and have some laughs was to reform The Filters. The first thing McConnell recalled doing was to ring Downie up about getting the band back together. Downie readily agreed but under one condition. "Gord said to me, 'I'll join the band again but I want Rob Baker in it as well.' Once we got on the road, it didn't take long to see how those two clicked."

This second go round was a harsh introduction to the realities of being in a band. Rather than simply ply the school dance circuit, this edition of The Filters would spend much of 1982 making ends meet outside of Kingston, on long drives to far-flung provinces and towns, often playing dives in front of small and often unappreciative crowds for little or no money.

McConnell, who often seemed to have a streak of gallows humor built into his mental makeup, explained just how bad the Filter excursions without understatement in *The Whig.com* article. "We played the dive bar circuit. We did the worst gigs together. It was like going to war."

And the war, according to Baker in *The Whig*

Standard, was beginning to take its toll. "We were playing Cornwall, Brockville, Bellville, a couple of gigs in upstate New York and a bunch of other places. The Filters were becoming more of a growing concern that Gord and I weren't prepared for. We just decided that we wanted to scale it back."

For Baker and Downie, the romance played out as a struggling band on a seemingly endless road to nowhere fueling this first real brush with music and the rock and roll life. But eventually the adrenaline rush gave way to no small amount of disappointment and despair. And an ever-increasing desire to get off the road and to return to the simpler times in Kingston.

Larry Stafford, who played in yet another Kingston band called Street Noise, and would later make a living as a top soundman, recalled in a *Whig Standard.com* conversation how he saw firsthand how the band reached their breaking point. "I remember going to see The Filters at some out of town dive. I went up to the room they were staying in, just to see how everybody was and they were all sitting on the floor. There was one mattress in the room and a rope attached to a wall that was a fire escape. The band was just sitting there. At one point, Gord looked to me and said…

…Is this as good as it gets?'"

Chapter Three
And So Hip Begins

The Tragically Hip came together in 1984 in a rather understated way. Downie, Baker and Sinclair, after a hard day of hitting the books at Queen's University, convened at Waldron Tower, a university residence building. There was some casual talk, a little strumming of guitar and some scat-like singing by Downie. At the end of it all, the trio agreed that it might be time to start a band.

Although two years younger than the others and still in high school, Johnny Fay's skills had made the rounds as a drummer talented beyond his years. "We had heard the rumors that there was this kid in high school who was a good drummer," Baker recalled in *The Whig Standard.* "So we sought out Johnny and brought him on board."

The band members to this day insist that their first musical adventure together was formed, quite simply, for fun and profit. But the reality was that, historically, the band would almost immediately be stepping out from the crowd. Punk was in a rapid decline and, to a large extent, had been replaced by fairly predictable and largely uninspiring commercial rock and pop. That they would be plying their trade, at least initially, in and around the city of Kingston would also be a challenge. There were very few venues for bands in those days and those were primarily the home of top 40 cover bands. Being a cover band would be easy.

But the band wanted to be more than that.

In a decision made early on, they decided to write a handful of originals and immediately make them a major portion of their live set. At least that was the popular consensus. But there is another school of thought regarding The Hip and original songs that insists it was all covers until mid/late 1985 when, it has been stated in many quarters that the song *Psychedelic Ramblings of Rich Kids* became the band's first original song to be featured in a live set. When it came to songwriting credit, the band was democratic despite the fact that Sinclair was given behind the scenes credit for several songs and, later sax player Davis Manning would receive some passing credit from the band for his songwriting efforts. Original material would typically be introduced to audiences as 'this is one of our own' or 'this is one of ours.'

In any case, songwriting from the band's inception was an organic, communal operation with Baker, Sinclair and Downie all having a hand in writing and arranging. As befitting their youthful outlook, those early songs were, primarily, rough, blues-based rockers. But even in those early days, while simple songs were the blueprint of the band, the members of the still unnamed and untried in a public setting The Hip, sensed an electricity and passion in their music, and that they would be able to take it somewhere special.

Two of the earliest Tragically Hip originals that came out of those sessions were *Baby Blueblood* and *Reformed Baptist Blues*. The former, dutifully chronicled in the must read *The Tragically Hip Unreleased Information Page*, contains the immortal lyric 'you can't maintain your champagne tastes on my beer salary' while the same site quotes Downie's take on *Reformed Baptist Blues* as "a song for anyone who goes to church strictly for the booze."

Once the band felt they were ready to perform, they looked to Queens University for their first gig. The school's student Fine Arts Group was planning on holding an event that would include musical entertainment. In short order the band with, as yet, no name, was on board for their coming out performance in November 1984.

In the spirit of the moment the band initially decided to call themselves the Bedspring Symphony Orchestra in homage to an old Rolling Stones bootleg album called Bedspring Symphony. But cooler heads prevailed when a skit from the Michael Nesmith (of Monkees' fame) television show called *Elephant Parts* included a plea for a charity for a fictional group called "The Tragically Hip." The absurdity of it all seemed to strike a tone with the band.

"We got to talking about The Tragically Hip and we thought that's a much better name," recalled Baker in the *Whig Standard*. "So we decided let's use that. In hindsight, we probably would have given it more thought. But the gig seemed like a one off thing. We didn't know if we were going to be a band beyond that one gig. We had to call ourselves something and The Tragically Hip seemed as good as anything."

Years later, Downie would add another element to the name mystery when he offered in a *Georgia Straight* interview that the term The Tragically Hip was also a part of a line in the lyrics to the 1982 song by Elvis Costello called "Town Crier" *(*"They're so teddy bear tender and tragically hip").

In any case, it would be The Tragically Hip that would make that fateful first concert appearance. It was a makeshift appearance to say the least. The band would have to rent a PA system for the occasion and cobble together songs by The Monkees, The Doors, The Yardbirds and The Rolling Stones.

"It was a terrible sounding room for a loud band," reflected Baker in a *Whig Standard* conversation. "We did three sets of tunes and in each set we did three original tunes."

But it was a start. The fledgling The Tragically Hip was willing to play any and all venues and the Queen's University student community would offer many opportunities to play out. But they were not in any rush. Sinclair related in the book *Have Not Been the Same: The CanRock Renaissance* that the band started out playing only one gig a month before progressing to weekend club appearances. "Only then did it start taking over what we were all doing because people started coming out."

Still others have offered a contradictory scenario in which The Hip, who were reportedly going under the name Weddings, Parties, Anything, played a lot of high school graduation dances and in any number of local taverns and clubs which had, to that point, never hosted live music before."

And once the band's willingness to play any and

all gigs, sometimes for free, sometimes for beer money, but rarely a lot, word got around. The Tragically Hip's viability (or profitability) had a number of area clubs and eateries clamoring for their services. Downie succinctly summed up the Kingston club scene when he told the *Queen's University Journal,* "There was always a gig and there was always somebody playing."

The Copper Penny Restaurant in Kingston, a regular haunt for Queens' University students, offered a fairly regular gig throughout 1985. Other shows during that period were the notorious Misty Moon in Halifax, the Kingston haunt The Lakeside Manor, Zorba's, Dollar Bill's and a campus bar named Alfie's (long since rechristened as The Underground), the later showcasing The Hip's willingness to literally play all night; sometimes chalking up three to four sets a night and playing as many as 50 songs.

From its inception, the band provided a heady dose of heavy drinking rock and blues style music. But, between the expectation of Stones and Clash covers, there were the occasional hip eccentricities often provided by songs by The Yardbirds, The Monkees and Elvis Presley among others. In a very early interview with *Queen's Journal,* Downie described what the band was doing at the time as "high energy dance music." Fay in the same conversation made the point of saying that The Tragically Hip were standing out from the glut of cover bands "by not playing the same songs everybody else was playing and that people were overdosing on."

Easily the most popular song in The Tragically Hip's early set was a little ditty called "The Bedrock

Song" from the classic cartoon *The Flintstones.* Conceived as more of a joke by Baker, "The Bedrock Song" became the most requested song in the band's sets, forcing the Hip to sometimes play the song three times in the course of a night. But that novelty aside, the band was making almost immediate strides in writing and performing new music.

Scratching out a meager living on the club circuit left the band open the suggestions from people that all covers was the way to go and that The Tragically Hip might make more money if they went out as a Doors clone band. The band's response was to write even more original songs. And the most prolific writer at the time would be Sinclair whose early efforts, the folk inspired "Times are Passing Us By" "Running for My Life" and "Waltz for Juliette" were quickly introduced into a set list that was slowly but surely evolving into a predominantly originals show.

Word was getting out that The Tragically Hip was more than just another Canadian bar band and, not surprisingly, that left even their earliest and most ardent supporters choosing up sides. Downie recalled the early perception of the band in the book *Have Not Been the Same*: *The CanRock Renaissance* that "Within Kingston, there were some who thought we were a university frat boy band while others thought we were working class bums."

Sinclair, Baker and Downie continued to plug away at respective degrees at Queen's University. Sinclair and Baker had pretty much buckled down and were nearing finishing their degrees. However, Downie seemed to have problems sticking with anything but his rock and roll dreams. By 1985, he had already gone through and given up on degrees in film and political science and was, arbitrarily, latching onto just about anything that sparked a passing interest. In a quote that appeared in *The Georgia Straight* and *Ear of Newt.com*, Downie conceded that "I did quite a tour of the various faculties but I didn't go to enough classes for any of it to rub off."

The Tragically Hip were constantly on the lookout for anything that would add substance to their basic rock and roll sound. Consequently it was not unexpected when the band decided to add a saxophone player to the band in 1985. What was a bit of a surprise was that they selected Davis Manning, a local musician of note in the Kingston area, who was 15 years older than the rest of the band.

Manning would turn out to be an important adjunct to The Tragically Hip, and more than just musically. He was a wise old hand when it came to how the rock and roll game should be played. He would be encouraging, driving home the point that it was in their long-term best interest to write their own songs. For the better part of a year and change everything and everybody seemed to click. The band was making progress and was inching ever closer to making some sort of living. But that's when things changed.

Manning and his girlfriend had carved out a nice relationship in Kingston and with The Tragically Hip beginning to make strides big enough to consider longer, farther reaching tours, Manning was suddenly uncomfortable with the idea of heading out on the road. Towards the end, Manning was becoming frustrated with his younger band members and questioning just how far this band could actually go.

"He was a good player and he pushed us a lot," Baker recalled in a *Whig Standard* interview with Sarah Crosbie, "but, in the end, his parting words to us he said, 'I can't put my life in the hands of a bunch of dumb college fuckers."

In the same article, Baker admitted some respect for Manning. "He had been there. He had done it all. He knew how it should be done and we were out there making all the mistakes, all the rookie mistakes we had to make."

Following Manning's departure, the band soldered on, playing a handful of local Kingston area gigs as a four piece. Without the texture afforded by the sax, The Tragically Hip were very much the rough and ready rockers. Noticeable was the ever-growing progression of Downie as the crazy, ranting, wild dancing and improvisational patter front man. During this period, Downie was much in his Iggy Pop element and the remainder of the band was quick to pick up on the vibe. Unorthodox transitions from song to song were often punctuated by left field, near poetic runs that the band was quick to pick up on. The covers carried more straightforward rock weight. But it was the new songs, and especially those with alternating instrumental and vocal shifts that were the most promising. The Tragically Hip was on the verge of flexing some mighty creative muscle.

But at the end of the day, the band finally agreed that a second guitarist sure would not hurt. And they did not have to look too far to find one.

Paul Langlois had decided in the early 80's that journalism and not music might be his calling and enrolled at Carleton University upon graduation from

KCVI. But the lure of the written word would not last long and he dropped out of Carleton. It would not be long before he got in touch with his old high school buddies Downie and Sinclair and moved into the apartment they were sharing. It was not long before the members of The Tragically Hip had reacquainted themselves with Langlois' guitar playing skills. But for the moment, Langlois was somebody to hang with and, occasionally, jam. But there was no immediate overture for their good buddy to join the band. But that did not mean that Langlois was not always around.

"Paul would come out to all of our gigs," Baker told the *Queen's University Journal*. "We'd be up on stage playing and Paul would be standing in front, dancing with the most beautiful girl in the bar." In the same interview, Sinclair jokingly acknowledged that the band was sweating their asses off while Langlois was reaping the benefits.

"So we decided to get him in the band just to spite him."

Letting a good buddy join the band was, in hindsight, a risk. As a guitar player Langlois was strictly an amateur. And the reality was that The Tragically Hip, still the local guys on the rise, had enough street cred to be able to entice an experienced guitarist to join the ranks. But, at the end of the day, the consensus was that the band wanted Langlois.

"Paul could play a few chords on the guitar," Baker remembered in a *Queens Journal* conversation. "But he wasn't very good. But we were like, 'He's got a great attitude and he's a great guy. Anyone can learn to play the guitar.

"It's not that hard."

39

Chapter Four
On the Road to Horseshoe

Langlois was officially introduced as a member of The Tragically Hip during a show in November 1986. He proved to be a quick study in all things musically Hip and had, after the inevitable bit of trial and error, easily assimilated himself into the working fabric of the band.

The band had eventually slipped away from 'the fun and beer money' attitude of that first year into a now, quietly driven stated goal of a professional career and stardom. The group was now willingly snapping up any available opportunity to play and be seen. A prime example being a late 1985 twin killing in which, after opening yet another campus related outdoor show for headliners Teenage Head, the band immediately packed their equipment and raced across Kingston in time to do a set at The Manor.

Along the way, The Tragically Hip would soon discover the reality of playing out. And that was that not all their shows would be Class A events. In fact, the members of the band would often recount the number of "shitty clubs" they appeared in, how they had to compete with rowdy drunks and a general lack of interest from an audience that, sometimes, numbered less than 20. But the band would not be discouraged and, in fact, became toughened in a *Road Warrior* sort of way to the challenges and bumps in the road.

Downie, in a *Nicholas Jennings.com* piece, remarked, "We play. We go where we're booked." Fay, in the same article, related that their relative youth and the kind of music they played made them a natural in a number of different venues. "We'd play the townie pubs, places like The Manor which was a biker bar. But we'd also play campus joints like Alfie's. We were local boys who were also students so we had a connection with both audiences."

Baker echoed Downie's penchant for hometown gigs when he told *Jam Canoe.com* "We played The Terrapin's Tavern, sweet 16 parties, high school dances, health clubs, a Jack and Jill party, biker picnics, anyplace we could play."

Baker would laughingly recall that while the band, in those days, would often walk away from an early gig with little or no money in their pockets, they had early on decided they were worth something for their efforts. "We set a very simple limit. As long as we walked away with $50 cash in our pockets and were allowed to drink for free, we'd play."

And they'd play a lot. Word of mouth and increasingly sold out clubs soon found The Tragically Hip averaging four to five gigs a week and each member walking away with $350. It was time for the band to make an important career choice. Baker and Sinclair had recently graduated from Queens University and Downie was continuing to flounder in his third year. It did not take much to convince Downie to drop out and give the band a go.

Sarah Harmer, a longtime friend of the band who would, years later, become quite the musician in her own rite and record with The Hip on the songs "Silver Road" and "Now for Plan A," recalled in a *Maclean's* conversation how she was introduced to the band by an older sister when she was 16 and, subsequently, became a regular at Hip shows back in the day. "Beginning around 1987, I'd see them at Nag's Head North in Toronto and Kincardine in Hamilton and a place called Call the Office in some beach town where they would usually play before a tiny crowd."

Harmer related that, even in those early days, The Hip were something special. "They were just so good at building an energy. They wrote different set lists for every show. They never just called it in."

But while the band often appeared professional beyond its years, the reality was that, in the mid 80's, The Tragically Hip really was not looking beyond the band being a conduit for a good time.

"We thought this was righteous money and it keeps us in beer, albums and pot," Baker told *Jam Canoe.com*, "so why would we stop doing it? Our feeling was let's just keep riding it and going as long as it's fun. We never did sit down and say 'Let's make this a career.' "

The band was ultimately encouraged the further they got outside the confines of Kingston. The tossup was either be a good old boys hometown band or risk it all in the world outside the city limits for the sake of hitting the big time. Into 1986, they were opting, more and more, for the later.

To that end, the band began sending roughly recorded demo tapes of their original material out to such disparate places as tour booking agencies and regional battle of the bands contests. But for all their efforts, the band members had to ultimately concede that, by their standards, not enough progress was being made and that they had most assuredly become complacent.

Sinclair said as much when looking back on those struggling times in an interview with *The Whig Standard*. "We were ready to go out there and take Toronto by storm. We didn't want to be bothered with The North Bay. But the reality was that, basically, we weren't a good enough band yet. We were spoiled in Kingston. We always played to packed houses and receptive audiences."

But their persistence and no small amount of networking finally paid off in August 1986.

A childhood friend of the band, Fraser Armstrong, who also served time as both the d*e facto* manager and roadie in The Tragically Hip's early days, thought he knew somebody who might be able to help. A former Kingston State Senator and Armstrong's brother-in-law named Hugh Segal. Indeed, Segal, who would occasionally run into the band's parents socially, did know somebody, a newly minted, since January of that year, management company founded by Allan Gregg and Jake Gold.

Segal recalled in a 2016 email conversation that "One summer day, Fraser handed my wife and I a tape and wondered if I might pass it on to Alan Gregg. Since we lived in Toronto, where Allan was based, Donna [Segal's wife] and I drove to Toronto and listened to the tape on the way home. My tastes run more toward the baroque so the music did not mean much to me. But Donna's appreciation of the music was more substantial than mine."

Upon reaching home in Toronto, Segal sent a courier with the tape enclosed across town to Gregg where it sat unopened for a number of days. The following Tuesday, Segal was chairing a top-level committee meeting when he received a note in the meeting room that said he had to speak with him urgently. Thinking it was something of a political nature, Segal went across the hall to Gregg's anteroom.

"Forgetting I had sent the tape, I walked into the anteroom and Alan said, 'I'm sorry to bother you Hugh, but The Tragically Hip is the best pure rock and roll band I've ever heard! How can I connect with them?' Having no idea what 'pure rock and roll revival' actually meant, I gave him the number that I had for Fraser."

What the two partners found upon listening to The Tragically Hip was an unexpected and quite pleasant surprise. The music, all originals, was very rough as befitting a low budget studio recording. But what they also found was a raw and dynamic sound and approach to the music that, immediately, got their attention. Gregg and Gold agreed that there was 'something' there. They also felt that, in order to cement their initial impressions, they would have to see the band perform live. That's when they called up the booker at a notorious Toronto Bar named Larry's Hideaway. The bar, which was legendary for its filthy, dirty and downright nasty vibe in which hard drugs were commonly consumed and prostitutes plied their trade in back rooms, was in the final months of existence when Gregg and Gold asked if there was any way The Tragically Hip could be a last minute add to a show.

Gold would recall in the book *Have Not Been the Same: The CanRock Renaissance* that "I called up the guy at Larry's Hideaway and said I need to see this band play next week and could I have them play on Saturday night? The guy said 'yeah, sure there's this Rolling Stones cover band playing.' I told him that was okay and that we just needed to see them play."

Gregg and Gold immediately got on the phone with the band who, quite understandably, were thrilled and readily set about rehearsing what would be a 40-minute set. On the day in question, the band made the two and a half-hour drive from Kingston to Toronto. On the surface, the gig had potential pitfalls. With a cover band headlining and a crowd primed to party, an unknown opening act, and one that would play original material, could well try an audience's patience. And despite The Hip's full intent to rock, the first couple of songs were reportedly treated with indifference. But by the end of the set, the crowd was on their feet and applauding, seeing and hearing exactly what Gold remembers experiencing in that dark and dank Toronto bar.

"The day I saw The Tragically Hip for the first time was the day the bar was set for me," he recalled in a quote that appeared in *Geocities.com* and *The Whig Standard*. "I remember to this day, Gord Downie opened his mouth and sang like three words and I said 'Oh my god!'"

The band signed on with Gregg and Gold literally on the spot.

45

Having the support and no small amount of clout was immediately evident. Gregg and Gold felt it was important to increase The Tragically Hip's touring horizon and were immediately on the horn to promoters and influential club owners to set up longer and wider ranging tours. Soon the limited opportunities in Kingston and nearby London were replaced by shows at such far-reaching locals as Toronto, Saskatoon, Ottawa and Winnipeg.

But in a sense they were standing still. Touring was still about long, crowded van rides with no roadies. It was 1986 but, as Faye related in a conversation with *The London Free Press*, it might as well have been back in 1984. "When we first started we would [typically] jump out of bed at 10:00 a.m., and drive for hours to a one shot gig in London. We would do three sets and an encore, hang out with friends for a while and then drive back to Kingston. We must have made that trip ten or 15 times."

And even though they had come a long way by 1986, and had management and all the trappings of a band on the rise, they were, in a sense, scratching at clubs that still required them to play covers. Earle Taylor, manager of the now defunct Kipling's Club where The Tragically Hip played numerous times, recalled in *The London Free Press* how the band chaffed, musically, when they played his club. "They performed a regular Monday to Wednesday set every six to eight weeks. They would play a lot of Doors' songs and they hated it."

But with Gregg and Gold guiding them, The Tragically Hip were soon moving up the ladder to more prestigious gigs. One of the most important being The Horseshoe Tavern in Toronto. The club, which has a primarily 'originals only' policy to this day, has played host to national touring acts as well as unknowns. The club's co-owner, Kenny Sprackman, related to this author in a 2016 interview that the first time The Tragically Hip played The Horseshoe Tavern was 1986.

"But it was not their first Toronto gig," Sprackman recalled. "That would have been The Isabella Hotel. They did that show in the hotel's basement."

Sprackman was involved in that show and, subsequently, was more than willing to give The Tragically Hip a shot at The Horseshoe Tavern. New acts typically started with Monday and Tuesday shows, then progressed to Wednesday and Thursday and, if the crowds they drew warranted it, they moved up to the often lucrative weekend gigs. Sprackman related that The Tragically Hip were an immediate success at The Horseshoe.

"From their very first shows, they were drawing at least 100 people. That was very good for an early to midweek band. But it quickly progressed to the point where they had people lined up out the door and down the street. The band shot up like a rocket."

Due, in no small part, to the fact that The Tragically Hip, when they played The Horseshoe Tavern, was a love fest both on stage and off. "They were not rock stars," said Sprackman. "They were gentlemen. They were good guys. They would hang out with the fans. They were definitely not egotistical people. They were people who loved to play music, who were grateful for the opportunity and were grateful to be there."

Sprackman was equally effusive on The Tragically Hip's talent. "The band, singularly and collectively are all great players." But the club owner singled out Downie for particular kudos when he recalled, "Lyrically and performance wise, Gord was incredible even in those early days. The early Gord was very spastic on stage. The man would sweat! By the time he got off stage, he would be soaked."

By his own estimation, Sprackman estimates that the band played The Horseshoe Tavern more than 20 times over the years and held a handful of record release listening parties at the club. Hip history also notes that it was after a show at the club in 1988 no less a personage than MCA Records President Bruce Dickinson was personally on hand to sign the band to a long-term recording contract.

Sprackman chuckled as he recounted that the historical moment was not necessarily the breathless way it had been explained in numerous articles.

"The reality was that the contract may well have been signed at The Shoe and that the MCA Records President may well have been in the audience that night," said Sprackman. "But the reality was that the A&R guy for MCA had already flown up and seen the band. They had been thoroughly scouted and seen and the process began here. Within four or five months of their existence on the bar scene, several record labels were aware of the band and a bidding war was, reportedly, shaping up. The actual signing of the band probably took ten minutes but there was a lot leading up to that."

Sprackman readily acknowledged that even in the early days, The Tragically Hip were beginning to lay down the roots of songs with a definite Canadian feel and that Downie was well on his way to his 'barstool bard' label. But he conceded that in those early days at The Horseshoe Tavern, the vibe was a little bit different.

"Their earlier stuff was a lot more rocky and hard-edged than what it would evolve into years later. Quite simply, in the beginning they were a rock band. But, even at that point, I was certain that they were going to become the next U2."

Chapter Five
Come Hip and Hells Angels

About the time The Tragically Hip was being courted by MCA, Gregg and Gold were preparing for the second phase in their development of the band. Which was to get some kind of record out, the better to court fans and that all-important radio airplay.

It seemed the appropriate time.

When not playing live, The Tragically Hip were constantly woodshedding new original songs. The reasoning being twofold: first, that the creative instincts within the band at that point were in a frantic, driven mode; hell-bent on getting out from under the 'cover band' image and, second, having the point constantly being driven home that original songs translated into commercial success and a long career.

To produce what was shaping up as an EP, the band turned to Ken Greer; a much credited producer/musician (the latter as guitarist for the Canadian group Red Ryder) who the band felt would be the ideal person to craft the band's rock and roll attitude with the subtlety of country, folk and pop accents. To test the notion, Greer and the band recorded a series of demo tapes in May 1986 that contained a number of Hip originals that included "Nuclear BBQ," "Leather Man," "It Came Around, I'm Okay" and "On the Shelf "(all songs that, to date, have never been released on a Hip album). The results were promising.

The self-titled *The Tragically Hip* EP was recorded late in 1986 at the Sounds Interchange, Phase One Studios in Toronto. And from the outset, the recording sessions were an exclamation point on The Tragically Hip's four years on the bar and club scene. All the songs had a rough, raw, very live and immediate quality to them, with Doors and Rolling Stones influences shooting through the seven songs that would ultimately make up the 27 minute EP. On the surface, to the casual listener, it would seem that the band's first foray into the recording studio was good, a bit tentative and somewhat predictable in spots, but a solid rock and roll effort. Even in those early sessions, it became obvious that the song "Smalltown Bringdown," with some obvious but effective Tom Petty accents, was the standout track.

Sinclair admits to having written "Smalltown Bringdown" at a very formative point in his life and, in a *Queens Journal* conversation, was believably passionate about the song. "I was a younger man, definitely looking beyond the borders of my hometown. I put that tune together with that youthful mentality that you're off to seek your destiny or whatever somewhere out in the world."

What was a bit unusual about this debut disc was that, unlike most EP's that tend to give the entire band writing credit, The Tragically Hip gave specific credit to individual songwriters. Bottom line being that

Sinclair and Baker seemed to have done the lion's share of the songwriting while Downie, seemingly the obvious lyricist of the group, received co-writing credits on only three of the seven songs.

Downie would later reflect on that first studio experience in the book *Have Not Been the Same: The CanRock Renaissance*. "The EP is a compilation of all the first things we did. We had a sentimental attachment to them and, in the studio, they wouldn't be anything but what they were. When it came time to decide who wrote what, that's what we did."

For a band with zero recording experience, the members of The Tragically Hip adjusted to Greer's to-the-point-instructions and a lightning production schedule that saw the entire album recorded in a week.

The initial plan for The Tragically Hip EP was a soft roll out in which a small run of albums, released on Gregg and Gold's imprint label, Rock Records, would be available for sale at shows and for promotional use. But word along the major label grapevine that The Tragically Hip was something special led to a representative of RCA hearing the tapes and wanting to do a deal with the EP. Gregg and Gold thought about RCA's proposal just long enough to realize that a licensing deal with RCA would guarantee distribution throughout Canada.

RCA was being basically hands off in their dealings with the band. Their lone request was that the band add two additional songs to what had originally been slated as a five song EP. As the band had recorded an additional 20 songs during the session, the additions would be no problem. But there would be a slight difference of opinion late in 1987. The

Tragically Hip EP was already mastered and, as dictated by RCA, would be released early in 1988. The only problem was that the band had told all their families and friends that the album would be out for Christmas. The Tragically Hip were bummed and an unhappy band was the last thing that Gregg and Gold wanted to deal with. "We were like shit!" Gold related in the book *Have Not Been the Same: The CanRock Renaissance*. "What are we going to do? The record company is telling us we can't just release the EP in Kingston. And we kept saying 'yes we can'."

Taking the bull by the proverbial horns, Gregg and Gold contacted all six of the record shops in Kingston and told them they would have copies of the EP and that they can be sold prior to RCA's scheduled release date. It was a daring move but one that would ultimately pan out as fans were alerted that there would be an early release in Kingston only. Needless to say, the EP immediately went number one in The Tragically Hip's hometown.

The album would have its formal release in a matter of weeks. Early reviews were decidedly mixed with some taking shots at the perceived immaturity of the band's songwriting while others took issue with less than subtle recording elements. But to a critic, The Tragically Hip were praised for their raw instrumentation and passion. And nobody could argue with the fact that what the band was laying down was a delightful throwback to pure rock that had, mostly, gone by the wayside in recent years.

Token attempts at getting on the charts with first "Smalltown Bringdown" and "Last American Exit" went for naught but there were enough Canadian stations, especially of the alternative rock nature, to get some airplay and, with a country-wide first legitimate tour about to begin, The Tragically Hip were primed for the big time.

Or so they thought.

Having top-flight management, a string of solid one-nighter club dates and an album out to boot gave them a leg up on most bands. But by the time the tour kicked off on January 1, 1988 in Kingston, there were little kinks in the persona of rock star. Early on, The Tragically Hip's set was honed to a solid mixture of largely originals and some covers. With each show, the band had seemingly become even tighter and Downie's turn as front man/madman was regularly the centerpiece of the largely encouraging reviews. But the reality was still long van drives, passable lodgings and the notion that they were still, more often than not, playing before less than packed houses.

Such was the case during a stop in Edmonton. "Last American Exit" had begun to make a bit of a buzz on the radio and the band were hoping to fuel it with a video for the song. The video was shaping up as a dark, introspective journey and the band was counting on a packed house to supply some stark footage. But when only ten people showed up at the club, the band had to alter the scope to a good but rather predictable 'band on the road' odyssey.

And then came Winnipeg. The Diamond Club was a well- known dance club that had made its bones on excellent DJ sets and the occasional appearance by a commercial pop or country act. And so it seemed like just about everybody was asleep at the switch when The Tragically Hip were booked into a week's worth of shows that included good money and a decent place to stay. There was only one problem...

...Their competition the night they played their first set at The Diamond Club was John Cougar Mellencamp who was performing across town and, apparently, drawing the same Tragically Hip kind of crowd. Consequently, The Tragically Hip played their first set to the club's bartenders and an empty house. Baker recalled what happened next in a *Jam.Canoe.com* story.

"No one was there so, at one point, Gord was laying on the stage singing and the manager of the club comes in, sees this and said, 'They're a punk band. No one told me they were a punk band.' He told his assistant that when they're finished, tell them they're fired."

The manager left. Not long after the Mellencamp concert let out, the band suddenly found themselves playing before a packed house of post-concert revelers. Their second and third sets of the night had a whooping and hollering crowd packing the dance floor and the band ending the night with three encores.

"When we finished the house guy came in and said, 'You guys are great, love your band, but you're fired'," recalled Baker. "Just like that, we had lost five gigs."

John Kendle, a local music critic familiar with The Hip but who was not in attendance at the show offered in a *Winnipeg Free Press* article that nobody was certain what happened that night. "The stories that I've heard differ. Some say that it had to do with the fact that someone spit on the stage at the band. Some say that it's because Downie performed a song while he was lying on the floor, which he was known to do."

The band woke up out in the wilds of Winnipeg with zero money and no immediate prospects. Downie recalled the foul mood experienced by the band the next morning in a *Winnipeg Free Press* story. "We came here, we got fired. We were looking at six nights of gigs gone. We were heading back to Kingston and becoming the accountants we always dreamed to be."

It was at that point that Kendle donned his guardian angel wings and literally saved the band's bacon. He, reportedly, contacted local booking agent Rob Hoskin who, in conjunction with the band's Toronto based booking agent, managed to piece together enough replacement gigs to fill out the lost days. Sinclair, in the book *Have Not Been the Same: The CanRock Renaissance*, related that help came from some very unexpected sources.

"The Hell's Angels came through and put us up at one of their hotels [Osbourne Village Motor Inn]. A local boxer, Donnie La Londe, had a bar called The Cornerboy's and he gave us a gig. It was not the most suitable place for a band but were out there and out of money so we were in no position to complain."

The up and down nature of that first extensive tour slowly but surely transformed the band into a songwriting machine with new tunes being churned out almost on a nightly basis. The Hip's blueprint remained an organic approach in which both communal and singular efforts serving as the jumping off point for creation. The songs *She Didn't Know* and *When the Weight Comes Down* were typical of The Tragically Hip's dark, introspective and insular side beginning to emerge. But it would remain for the songs *"New Orleans is Sinking"* and *"38 Years Old"* to effectively mix and match American based blues and an erudite yet humane slice of history and autobiography that would be an important step in the band taking on the mantle of Canadian storytellers. And it would be the moment when Downie truly stepped out from behind the shadows unleashing his lyrical and surreal style of storytelling for the first time.

The tour would also succeed in kicking open the door of commercial acceptance. The Tragically Hip had been doing fairly well for a first time record by a largely unknown band. Airplay continued to be a rollercoaster ride; with rare exceptions Hip songs getting only sporadic play amid the prevailing hit makers of the day. But with more and more people experiencing The Tragically Hip live, the more established FM and Alternative outlets were giving the likes of *Smalltown Bringdown* and *Last American Exit* a more expansive shot on their playlists. The band's originality and just plain musical smarts was beginning to pay off.

The initial deal with RCA was for one year; a test run to see if the label saw a future with the band. Midway through their first Western Canada tour in 1988, the contract was coming to an end and both sides seemed anxious to negotiate a long-term extension. Every element of a proposed new deal seemed agreeable to both sides. Until RCA came up with one requirement that The Tragically Hip could not tolerate.

"The label told us that they wanted use to change our image," Baker said in *Jam Canoe.com.* "They told us they wanted us to dress up in fringe jackets and be a country rock band because that was supposed to be the next big wave. We didn't agree and so we walked away from the deal. Now I can't believe we even had that conversation."

Throughout the remainder of 1988, The Tragically Hip were a literal blur of activity. Their initial tour would last well into September. New material was being created while a definite style and tone was being crafted. Experience in front of live audiences, under conditions good and bad, had resulted in a very real musical identity.

Toward the end of the year, the aforementioned show at The Horseshoe Tavern resulted with MCA President Bruce Dickinson signing the group to his label. Dickinson had his own plans for The Tragically Hip. He was a meat and potatoes executive who believed in hard work. He told the group upfront that he did not think they would have a lot of hit singles but, rather, would build a following through solid albums and constant touring.

The Tragically Hip would prove him wrong.

Chapter Six
Up to Here in Hip Hits

By their own estimation, The Tragically Hip had played more than 300 gigs by then, many of them whose conditions the band members made no bones about being "shitty". The crowds were, often, indifferent and sometimes totally turned off to what the band was doing. For The Tragically Hip, it was a time, emotionally and creatively, of digging deep and heading in a new direction and parts unknown.

It was the perfect time for the band to record what many observers would later look back on as their most provocative and thought-provoking statement, the album *Up To Here*.

Sinclair recalled in the book *Have Not Been the Same: The CanRock Renaissance* how their dues paying days on the road had matured them as musicians and men. "The humility of playing in shitty clubs night after night made us a better band. It was up to us to internalize what we were doing and let the songs speak for themselves."

And what the latest batch of songs was saying was look deeper and darker, look to an amalgamation of history, fact and fantasy and, at the band's soul, look back on Kingston and, by association, all the mental and emotional T's and I's that could be crossed and dotted in telling stories that would impact psyches and create new memories.

Truth was very much the watchword when The Tragically Hip signed with MCA Records. And truth was very much on their plate when they sat down to discuss where they would record *Up To Here* and who would, creatively, pilot the ship. To draw on the best possible soul/blues/dirty rock vibe, the band selected the legendary Memphis studio, Argent Studios. Don Smith was chosen to pilot the project and nobody could argue with the choice. Smith, whose talents transcended genres and performers, was of particular interest to The Tragically Hip because of working association with the likes of Tom Petty & The Heartbreakers, Bob Dylan, The Travelling Wilburys, Keith Richards, Stevie Nicks and The Rolling Stones and for his ability to alternately prod and hand hold musicians as he attempted to get through to the soul of the players and the project.

Smith and The Hip would have some preliminary conversations, with the band taking the lead on how and where they wanted *Up To Here* to go. While recording The Tragically Hip EP had been a joyous adrenaline rush, the band insisted on more time for *Up To Here*. "There had been planning," Downie explained to *The Chicago Tribune*. "We had been writing for the occasion. We took a nice, measured amount of time and did it."

The leisurely approach continued once recording began. Casual visitors to the studio would often be confronted by a workshop atmosphere in which Smith and the band would be woodshedding ideas around a table full of beer cans, with good natured back and forth being the order of the day. However, Downie would tell *The Chicago Tribune* that, ultimately, there was method to the madness.

"Don was getting into the sounds we were happy with. We would spend a lot of time tuning drums and getting the right microphone settings. Don was very keen about getting the right sounds for the band. But when that was done, the approach was to turn on the tape machine and let us roll, let us play."

The result was an amalgam of styles. The album was rock but it was rock with a sense of smarts, experimentation and subtle nuances. Songs like "Blow at High Dough," "New Orleans is Sinking" and "38 Years Old" were almost literary and rough-hewn intent. One can only speculate what the studio sessions were like that produced these moments. Downie, ever the subtle and to the point exponent, explained to *Tear of Newt.com* that, "We made this album to fit our own standards. We raised the bar pretty high."

Timing was everything when it came to releasing *Up To Here*. The band's constant touring and the moderate success of their EP had set in motion a Tragically Hip climate of anticipation in which the group, already high on the good will ambassador list for Canada, were slowly being talked about as a national treasure. Although MCA had already slotted *Up To Here* for an August/September release, they were smart enough to prime the pump when, in April 1989, they released the album's first single, "Blow at High Dough."

As a first single, "Blow at High Dough" was

fairly unexpected. It's down home, Canada-centric philosophy of 'don't walk before you can crawl' had its charms. Done up rock style, it seemed catchy enough for a first radio strike.

CBC Music.com caught up with Downie long enough for the singer to admit that *Up To Here* signaled a new stage for the band and that the element of timing was very much part of their template. "We hit the Canadian music scene when the winds of change were blowing. Ten years ago we probably wouldn't have gotten away with doing what we do now."

"Blow at High Dough" would take the honor as The Tragically Hip's very first charted single in Canada, peaking on the RPM Singles Chart at No. 48 and going all the way to No. 1 on the RPM Canadian Content Chart. The good news would be received by the band on the road.

After what must have been a fairly short break following the completion of *Up To Here*, the band, by June, was back on the road, hitting such familiar stomping grounds as Ontario (gigs at Mather Arch and Harris Park) and Toronto (CNE and Eastern Sound Studios) while, occasionally making their way across the border for another crack at expanding their base into the US. Of the latter, July 7, 1989 gig at the O' Cayz Corral in Madison, Wisconsin would be memorable. That night, The Tragically Hip would headline in front of an audience estimated at 40 people. What made the show equally surreal was that their opening act was yet another new band on the block...Nirvana.

Through the summer months, The Tragically Hip

were working fairly predictable territory. Lots of touring, sometimes visiting cities they had passed through countless times before. Despite their constant road presence and a second album about to be released, The Tragically Hip had become a fairly well-known presence on the Canada music scene and, just as often, still an unknown quantity. They were still hitting their share of 'shitty' places, playing before crowds that, occasionally, numbered in the low two digits.

But now they had the advantage of having radio at their back and, in the case of "Blow at High Dough," a song that was having massive staying power in the minds and hearts of listeners. Typically, after three months, a second single would already have been dropped. But, in the case of The Hip, it did not seem necessary. Because the song continued to hang in on the charts and the radio. "Blow at High Dough" was the rock and roll equivalent of the little engine that could.

The promise of *"Blow at High Dough"* and the reported rave reviews of the band's live performances of their new material was fully realized on September 5 when *Up To Here* was officially released. One thing was quickly evident. Despite a more diplomatic tone that credited the entire band as songwriters, there was immediate evidence that Downie had, creatively, stepped up as a centerpiece.

Downie had always been literate, well-read and a person who praised and revered history and small moments in time. The band's second single, "New Orleans is Sinking" was typical of Downie and the band's evolving attitude. The song, a loosely based jam session, appeared, to many listeners, to take a sonic, gauze-filtered fantasy look at catastrophes real and imagined interspersed with a Downie lyrical aside or impromptu slide into another song at a mid-song break. Typical of the band's approach to 'workshopping' new material in a live setting, "New Orleans is Sinking" almost immediately became a set must from its inception and paved the way for the single to be a smash upon release.

"New Orleans is Sinking" almost immediately upon its November release peaked at a respectable No. 70 on the RPM Canadian Singles Chart, No. 1 at the RPM Canadian Content Chart and, perhaps most telling for The Tragically Hip's long term plans for international stardom, the song cracked the US Billboard Mainstream Rock Tracks Chart at an encouraging No. 30.

As for the album, *Up To Here* was aces in Canada. *Up To Here*, almost immediately, hit No.14 on the Canadian Contact Album Chart. The album would go Canadian gold in two months (Jan. 1990) and Canadian platinum by March. Despite a good showing on *Billboards*' Album Tracks Chart, The Tragically Hip continued to struggle in the American listening consciousness, rising no higher than a tepid 170 on the *Billboard* Top 200 Album Chart.

Up To Here had captured Canadian listener's fancy with a creative left turn. Still a solid rock album, the band had chosen as its voice a largely introspective and often bleak pallet in which a crosshatching of American and Canadian blues experiences pointed at a universal small town sense of frustration. Songs like "38 Years Old," which chronicled a downbeat aftermath of a well-documented Kingston prison experience, and *Opiated* which hinted at a small town Ontario experience where the only hope from an unhappy real life was drugs, pointed toward the group taking a much larger step away from the credo of sex, drugs and rock and roll.

While their album continued to sell a ton in Canada, The Tragically Hip continued to slog it out in America where their relative obscurity in the States resulted bringing flashbacks to their struggling days touring in Canada. Langlois explained the dichotomy while playing the US in a conversation with *The Chicago Tribune*.

"We recently played to an audience of four people in a Bloomington, Indiana college town pub. But that show turned out to be one of the best shows on the tour. We just said, 'Why not?' We've had so many shows like that in Canada anyway. We just decided to go ahead and have a good time despite the small crowd. And all four people in the audience stayed until the very end."

But the tour would also have its down side.

Journalist Meighan O'Brien recalled in a *CBC News* article how when, on assignment from a local magazine, she wandered into the iconic New York club CBGB's to review and interview a band she had never heard of before... a reportedly up and coming Canadian band called The Tragically Hip.

"The bar was empty when they started playing. I was the only one. And then people started to come in. People started to walk in, but they weren't leaving, they were staying. And it got more crowded and more crowded and more crowded and more crowded and every song they played, people got more enthusiastic and started roaring and cheering."

O'Brien stayed until the last song and later met up with the band for the interview and, as it would turn out, hours of breakfast chat and pool games before she said her goodbye early the next morning and returned to her room. Her eyes had barely closed when her phone rang. It was Gord.

"Gord asked, 'if we could help them out?'" she recalled. "I said 'Sure. What's up?' He said 'Our van got stolen.'"

O'Brien said the band could wait in her room while their manager dealt with the calamity. In due course there was a knock on the door and the members of The Tragically Hip trooped into her room. O'Brien related the look she saw on their faces.

"They were all very sad men."

Chapter Seven
Hip is What You Make It

But the band survived the loss of the van, as well as some very valuable antique equipment, and celebrated the New Year and were soon well on the road into 1990 where *Up To Here* continued to treat them well. A second and third single (*Boots or Hearts* released in February 1990 and "38 Years Old" in April 1990) did consistent business and ended up at No. 41 on the RPM Singles Chart. America had been a whole different story. Neither *Boots or Hearts* or "38 Years Old" cracked the Billboard charts and *Up To Here* would sell a tepid 10,000 albums in the USA during its first year.

Even at this early stage of The Tragically Hip's career, music critics, social observers and pop culture pundits were offering up a myriad of reasons why the land across the border was so slow in coming around. Canadians who have become famous in America first had to move there to take advantage of opportunities while The Hip, early on, took great pains to align themselves with the notion that they were Canada's band and Canada was their birthplace. Others pointed out that the band's songs were largely Canadian in lyric and influence and were difficult for Americans to digest as something that could be American centric. Then there was the old saw of a corporate owned industry whose music playlist was populated by safe stars and programmed musical styles; something The Tragically Hip were not.

Even in their salad days, The Hip were already dealing with why their music was so Canada-influenced and why they could not crack the US market. It had gotten to the point that even the normally unflappable Downie once bristled at the question during a conversation with the *BBC News.* "Interviewers always ask us about our success or lack of success in the States, which I find absurd. While that is a story of the band, there are so many other stories."

But truth be known, by the time The Hip captured their very first Juno award in 1990 for Most Promising Artist, the band was already hopelessly entrenched as a Canadian band in music, heart and soul. They lived and breathed Canada and, over the years, would actively court that reputation.

By the time, *Up To Here* was well on its way to selling a reported 200,000 copies in a matter of months, The Tragically Hip were back to doing what they did best, which was to tour. The shows in places like Windsor, Toronto, Halifax and Vancouver had become bigger and 20 or more song sets had become the norm. But the band would take small steps in their continued efforts to expand beyond Canada's borders, doing US shows in Buffalo and Houston and, in a first step in true international conquest, made a quick stop in Rotterdam, Holland to headline a sold-out show.

The Tragically Hip's live show had long since evolved into an organically driven scene, electric in execution and presence. The Hip had always had the reputation of being nice guys and, on stage in the early days, maybe just a bit passive, preferring to let the power of the songs carry the day. But the 1990 tour would see The Hip turning a corner, capable of a monster performance that would regularly drive the audience to distraction...

...Or, as described by Baker in a *Georgia Straight* interview from back in the day, much worse. In particular, the New Years' Eve show in Vancouver in which the audience threw beer cans at the band and an overzealous fan dumped a jug of unknown liquid on Downie. "It was a good crowd. It got a little hairy a couple of times, but that's okay. We don't encourage people to throw things at us but we don't take it personally when they do."

But the guitarist concedes that the 1990 Canadian tour did have its moments and that, personally, the band was not inclined to put a damper on their fun. "The last time across Canada we had a few bad incidents, two in Calgary and one in Edmonton. Someone broke their neck at one of our gigs. Mostly its stage jumping but, this time, somebody climbed way up into the scaffolding and fell off. And the last time in Ottawa was pretty bad too. We had about 30 people taken out in stretchers. I don't know what you can do about people jumping off the stage. They want to show their enthusiasm and we don't want to put a damper on them."

Throughout 1990, the band continued to take every opportunity to write, already anxious to get new music out there and to improve on the success being generated by *Up To Here*. The Hip were true believers in the process of creative growth and never seemed to look back for long and always with an eye toward the future. An upcoming album would be more of the same.

Early on, Hip songwriting sessions operated in what would best be described as a separate but equal universe. Downie would often be found sitting in a corner by himself, notebook open and jotting down random lyrics. Meanwhile the remainder of the band would be laying down musical grooves. When something on the musical end seemed to work, the group would run it by Downie who, in turn, would thumb through his notes and come up with something that would fit the groove.

"The songs [we were writing at that point] were much more of a collective effort which is something we've been working toward since the beginning," Baker explained to *The Georgia Straight*. "We're probably better players and better songwriters than on the last album."

Baker's last point struck home midway through 1990 when The Hip, literally in the middle of a grueling odyssey across Canada, were turning out songs like "Anchor on a Thread", "Scathed," "Not So Necessary," "Montreal" and "If You Lived Here"; songs that to, this date, have gone unreleased but were showing signs of a band delving roughly and deeply into more ambitious ground. By September, The Tragically Hip were ready to come off the road and head into the studio.

In a *Road Apples* odyssey, recalled by the band

(not individually identified) in *The Hip.com*, The Hip related that "With *Road Apples* we had the benefit of working with producer Don Smith and engineer Bruce Barris again. We still had plenty to learn about studios and it made sense to team up with these guys. We really enjoyed working with them last time and there would be one less unknown [a new producer] in the recording equation."

Sinclair would echo those sentiments in conversation with *CBC Music*. "We were kind of clicking our heels to work with Don Smith again. It was kind of no pressure, to have as much fun as possible."

The next step was to book a studio that would be conducive to a free and easy recording atmosphere. They settled on the Kingsway Studio, settled right in the middle of The French Quarter in New Orleans, located, literally, in the middle of an old mansion, complete with 14 foot high ceilings and quite natural acoustics.

The overriding intent of the *Road Apples'* sessions was to reproduce what The Tragically Hip sounded like live, rocking, raw and with a large dose of passion. This goal was aided by the fact the band was able to capture the vibe of New Orleans and recycle those wild and disparate elements into their music. "New Orleans is a lively town and we're sure the whole vibe of the city is on this record," the band said in *The Hip.com*. "We were really working hard and were totally inspired by the city. *Road Apples* is probably a grittier, more urgent sounding recording than Up To Here."

During the five-week session, the band could regularly be found playing in an enormous room, large enough for the entire band to create a primarily live sound. Instrumentally speaking, The Hip were more than up to snuff. Baker's riffs were alternately thick and searing and moved savagely with Sinclair's mighty bass bottom. Langlois and Fay added constant driving patterns and an assured backbeat. But it would be Downie's lyrical take that would turn *Road Apples* into something compelling and smart.

If The Hip were designing *Road Apples* as a vehicle for cracking the US market, they were seemingly committing commercial suicide. For while, musically, the album was chock full of good old meat and potatoes rock and roll, lyrically the disc was full to overflowing with Canada centric themes and literary asides. Downie was exercising his intellect. To wit: the song "Three Pistols" was dedicated, in large part, to the popular Canadian painter Tom Tomson. The provincial symbol of Quebec makes unbridled reference. "Born in the Water" talks Canadian politics when it takes on the controversial Meech Lake Acord debate. "Remembrance Day" addresses the always sexy topic of the Canadian commemoration day for its war dead. And finally the song "Cordelia" weaves a stirring rock anthem about the third daughter of King Lear.

But amazingly, the mixture of hard rock, with occasional folk elements and Downie's highbrow lyrics, augurs into a stirring musical experience. The album was completed in early October and the consensus of those who heard the tapes was that it was easily the best Hip album to date.

Now all they had to do was figure out what to call it. Several names were tossed around and quickly discarded. At one point they thought very seriously about calling the album Saskadelphia. The band, via their *The Hip.com* website, recalled the reason why Saskadelphia struck an emotional chord. "It reflected, we thought, aspects of our life on the road, the 'where the hell are we now' feeling you can get near the end of a long tour."

"It was actually a funny story," Baker related to *The Georgia Straight*. "Our American label [Sire] felt that all of our titles were too much inside jokes, or that they sounded too Canadian. And they were really giving us this 'Oh no, Americans won't understand it.'"

Needless to say that Sire's digging in their heels on the name of the album had begun to annoy the band and, by association, the group's devotion to their Canadian heritage. "So we said, 'Okay, how about *Road Apples*. And of course the label in Los Angeles had no idea what Road Apples were. They said 'Oh yeah! Songs you wrote on the road! We love it.' What they did not know was that Road Apples was slang for horseshit. So in a way we ended up calling the album horse shit as a little jab at the folks that didn't like Saskadelphia."

The irony was that when *Road Apples* was released in February 1991, it was anything but horseshit.

"Little Bones", a straight-ahead blues rocker bolstered by Downie's dramatic vocals, was an immediate hit, debuting at No. 11 on the Canadian Top 100 Singles chart. The album, bolstered by a flood of positive and, yes, thoughtful reviews, almost immediately landing in the upper reaches of the RPM's Top 100 Album chart and, by April, hitting No. 1, the first Hip album to reach the coveted top spot. Two more singles, "Three Pistols" peaking at No.

59 on the Canada Singles chart, No. 11 on Canadian Content chart and, a happy surprise, a respectable No. 43 on the US Mainstream Rock chart, and "Twist My Arm," No. 22 on the Canadian Singles list and No. 3 on the Canadian Content listing, followed. A small bit of Hip trivia surrounding "Twist My Arm" was that the B-side of the single, a live version of "Highway Girl" from The Hip's EP, would become a minor hit on Canadian radio as well.

However, the failure of *Road Apples* and the band's singles (save "Three Pistols") to make the slightest dent on US radio had the band in a quandary. The Hip enjoyed playing the States and would often look back fondly on many of their US tour stops. But the continued reluctance on stations to play their music was frustrating. If The Tragically Hip had followed the path of fellow Canadians, The Barenaked Ladies, guitarist Baker admitted that the band's fortunes might have been different.

"Before The Barenaked Ladies had their hit [in the States], they toured nonstop for two years down there," he told *The Georgia Straight*. "That's a huge commitment. The reality is that we all have families and I'm not anxious to lose my family."

But when it came time to do the *Road Apples'* tour, the band continued to give the US yet another shot, scheduling a full half dozen stateside stops in the middle of the expected litany of Canadian gigs. These tour stops were conspicuous by the band's tendency to switch up sets and, with Downie taking the lead, alternately tense and manic theatrics.

A stop at Coyotes in Tucson, Arizona showcased The Hip in an intense mood and, to many who were collectors on a thriving bootleg circuit, is considered one of their best early gigs. A Hollywood California show at The Roxy saw the band at their improvisational best with what can best be described as 'different' takes on the songs "New Orleans is Sinking" and "Highway Girl."

The tour was also newsworthy, and perhaps a bit surprising considering their low visibility factor outside of Canada, by a series of mid and late tour excursions to Europe, that included The Pink Pop Festival in Holland (where the band played in front of an estimated 300,000 people), The Paradisio in Amsterdam and Batschkapp in Frankfurt, Germany. The response to those shows were enthusiastic and gave credence that, despite continued lackluster sales response in the United States, The Tragically Hip, whose continued success in Canada, gave them literal carte blanche to do what they wanted musically, decided it was time for a change.

The band's relationship with Sire Records in the US had been rocky from the beginning and radio in the States had been less than friendly in Canada. So while they had found pockets of support for their live shows and would continue to play in the US, the feeling by the band was that The Tragically Hip had become a minor cog in the marketing machine. And so, not long after *Road Apples* had literally tanked in America, the band officially ended their deal with Sire.

There was a sense of relief and excitement in the decision. They felt free to explore other possibilities. And to their way of thinking, the next stop was the rest of the world.

But 1992 would bring trouble in paradise.

Chapter Eight
A Bitter Pill to Swallow

Road Apples would sell approximately 300,000 albums during its first year. But its inability to sell anything in the United States continued to frustrate the band. There were also other things to consider.

While The Tragically Hip's trademark guitar heavy blues rock sound continued to be a draw in a live setting, radio stations that would take heavy rock under consideration were now gravitating toward a more polished sound. It would remain to be seen if The Tragically Hip could play by those rules.

Further intrigue surrounding the band during that period would surface in 2010 centered on hints that recording *Up To Here* had opened up some ego and creative difficulties within the band's much publicized solidarity. In an expansive University of Saskatchewan master's thesis by Paul David Aikenhead entitled *Man Sized Inside: A History of the Construction of Masculinity in The* Tragically *Hip's Album Fully Completely*, Aikenhead, during lengthy discussions with the band, was told by the always candid Baker that the vibe during the recording of *Road Apples* was nothing if not shaky.

"Little politics and intrigues entered into it," quipped Baker. When pressed by Birkenhead, Baker would disclose that, sometime during the recording of *Road Apples*, Downie announced that he would no longer sing other people's lyrics. Whether or not Downie's pronouncement influenced *Road Apples'* increased Canada centric lyrics is not certain. What is certain, according to Baker, was that there was suddenly tension in the band. "It was a bitter pill to swallow." But, ultimately, the band realized that it was in their long-term best interest that Downie develop as a lyricist and performer.

The shake out process of this new order of writing songs would become evident when the band began writing songs that would, ultimately, be included in their next album, *Fully Completely*. The majority of the songs were written and recorded in demo form at the house of record store owner, Jonathan Sugarman and in the Toronto rehearsal space of another Canadian band, The Cowboy Junkies. The process was communal to say the least with the band forming a circle at the beginning of each session and bounce musical and lyrical ideas off each other. Downie, who was just now testing his mantle of band lyricist out, would often find himself frustrated at the rest of the band coming up with a riff that would, immediately, end with the singer running off to a stack of note paper to come up with the appropriate lyric.

Short term, MCA Records was beginning to get impatient with the band's lack of US success and was strongly making recording suggestions which the band seemed, hesitantly, inclined to go along with. For openers, a different producer, Chris Tsangarides.

Tsangarides had long ago become the go to producer when it came to hard rock and heavy metal bands looking for a radio friendly tune up. Tsangarides had proven his 'metal' on a long string of albums by the likes of Black Sabbath, Judas Priest, Thin Lazy and Yngwe Malmsteen. The producer had taken a shine to The Tragically Hip and took it upon himself as a challenge to create the band's powerful, live sound in a studio setting. The members of The Hip knew the producer by reputation and seemed willing to give it a shot. Even if it meant travelling to London and Tsangarides' Battery Studios to record.

But as Baker recalled in a *Globe and Mail* interview, "The making of *Fully Completely* was about us wanting to learn. For us, bringing in a process is surrendering to the process and letting someone else take charge. It's very hard to give up any part of your fiefdom."

Tsangarides had a very by the book, almost militaristic style of producing a record and the band soon became part of that experience. Battery Studios was located in a very desolate, out of the way location in London. The hotel the band would stay in was, likewise, figuratively speaking, far away from any off hours distractions or entertainment. Downie recalled the sense of isolation the band experienced in London in the book *Have Not Been the Same*. "We stayed in a real depressing hotel in a nothing area of London and then would go off to another depressing area of London to work." When not working, the band would while away their free time playing soccer in a nearby park, watching television, playing scrabble and doing a whole lot of drinking.

All of which made Tsangarides' approach to recording seem even more real and contrary. The producer had made his creative bones by literally deconstructing a band's music and then putting together each track, instrument by instrument from the ground up. The first three weeks of the sessions saw the entire band playing but only the drums being recorded. The process repeated itself in week four with only the bass being recorded. Guitars were recorded over a three days period in week five and, finally, the last three days of the session were set aside for the recording of all the vocals. When it came time for Tsangarides to mix the project, the band was nowhere to be found.

But, despite suddenly dealing with a totally different kind of recording process that, admittedly, at times would appear disorienting to the band, Downie insisted in *Ear of Newt.com* that recording *Fully Completely* was one big good vibration. "It was the same sort of principles as with the previous albums in the sense that we were all chipping in and conjuring up things and trying out different things in those sessions. There seemed to be no tension involved. This seemed to be completely devoid of that and it was probably because we had the songs so well fitted."

Fully Completely was scheduled for an October 6, 1992 release date. But those who had managed to get an advanced listen were already trumpeting the album as a major turning point in the evolution of the band. Tsangarides' approach to mixing and matching the music had turned out to be nothing less than a sonic musical tapestry in which rough edges and more subtle sounds created a more mature sounding kind of rock and roll within the established Tragically Hip framework. But it did not take long for observers to settle on the band's new centerpiece. Now lyrically free, Downie was spreading his poetic, literary and highbrow style of songwriting in a decidedly Canadian direction, painting word pictures of well-known and small moments of Canadian stories within a rock and roll framework in the context of easily half of *Fully Completely* songs.

Unless they were serious about Canadian history and famous news stories, the significance of *Fully Completely* subject matter might have easily escaped the listener. But for Canadians, even those already attuned to The Tragically Hip being the next big thing, the album pretty much sealed the deal. "Courage (For Hugh MacLennan*)* " referenced the Canadian author and was lyrically driven by his influential novel *The Watch that Ends the Night*. "Looking For a Place to Happen" waved an opinionated finger at the European encroachment into indigenous Canadian lands. "At the Hundredth Meridian" explores the line of longitude that separates Western Canada from the Central and Atlantic regions. The Hip's lifelong love of hockey made its presence felt in the song "Fifty Mission Cap", the career and death of Toronto Maple Leaf's player Bill Barilko, while their sense of justice gets an emotional workout in "Wheat Kings", the story of Canadian David Milgaard who spent 23 years in prison after being falsely accused of rape and murder.

The consensus was that *Fully Completely* was a Canadian album for Canadians and that The Tragically Hip were riding a growing tide of nationalist pride and identity. But the band members were quick to defend their effort as anything but.

Downie, in a conversation with *QCBC* podcast denied that there was any deliberate attempt at patriotic intent and that he was just writing about what he knew. "That was really freeing, edifying to be able to do that," he explained. "It seemed like a whole world was opened up to anybody that wanted to write about such things. It had been a closed wing of the house that you really didn't go to if you were serious about making it."

Guitarist Baker echoed those sentiments during a conversation with *Man Sized Inside* thesis author Aikenhead when he offered, "There are certain Canadian references in the work but I think Gord has always thought in much wider, larger terms. In a strange way it is easily misinterpreted. I don't think he [Downie] considers himself a great patriot."

Whatever people were thinking, the reality was that, upon release, *Fully Completely* was an immediate smash in Canada. There was an expected rush of sales that exceeded 150,000 copies right out of the box and would climb to 200,000 copies by January '93 that pushed *Fully Completely* to No. 1 on the Canadian Album chart. The first single, "Locked in the Trunk of a Car", showed promise, landing at No. 11 on the Canadian charts. The follow up single, "Fifty Mission Cap," would top out at No. 40. Perhaps the biggest surprise was that a third single, "Courage," not only climbed to No. 10 on the Canadian Singles chart but managed a hefty No. 16 on the *Billboard* US rock tracks chart.

The band was hopeful that this album would be the one to break through in America. But behind the scenes, there were signs that all was not well in corporate MCA. Bruce Dickinson, MCA president, who had championed the band from the beginning, had suddenly, depending on which story you believe, either been ousted from his position or quit shortly after the release of *Fully Completely*; leaving many of the departments and agendas in disarray. The Hip began hearing the stories but, perhaps, the runaway success of *Fully Completely* in Canada, had distracted them from the upcoming early in 93 US release.

Sinclair, in the book *Have Not Been the Same: The CanRock Renaissance*, would recall the moment when reality hit The Hip hard. "We were still holding out for the equivalent American success for the album. Then two weeks before the US release, we found out that MCA had cut off all the US promotion budget for the record. All the record company would say 'it's gonna be big boys! Look out!' Then the week after that, no one was returning our calls. That's the way it was."

Chapter Nine
Another Roadside Attraction

Nineteen ninety-three was starting out as a year to forget. The Hip were upset at once again having their US hopes dashed. Gregg and Gold were downright pissed. Things were reportedly getting nasty as the band attempted to change the scenery. When the dust settled, the band remained with MCA for their Canadian label but would, subsequently, sign with Atlantic Records for US distribution.

But The Tragically Hip were nothing if not realists and the reality was that they still had an album that was going gangbusters in Canada and it was time to get on the road to support it. But this tour would be something special. Almost from the outset, the band had been big on supporting other Canadian talent and would rarely say no to doing a show that would benefit a worthy charity. The band came up with the idea of combining their love for the old style travelling rock and roll shows while exposing other talented musicians with a series of mid tour shows called Another Roadside Attraction.

With so much Canadian talent to consider, The Hip came up with a solid touring lineup that included

Crash Vegas, Hothouse Flowers and Daniel Lanois. However, The Hip would use the occasion of Another Roadside Attraction to add a superstar act from Australia, Midnight Oil.

On the surface it seemed like a good match. Both bands were politically and socially active and it showed in their music. Upon meeting, Midnight Oil front man Peter Garrett also found that they were very cool people. Which, Garrett offered in a conversation with *Maclean's*, were the main reasons why his band, which had been a headlining act in North America for some time, agreed to be a glorified opening act for the Another Roadside Attraction shows.

"Our attitude has always been that we don't open for anybody and, except for an early date opening for The Ramones, we never did. We didn't look at the offer so much as opening for them as it was we were joining them on tour. It was an opportunity to broaden out and play with a band that we felt some kind of affinity. That doesn't always happen."

The *Fully Completely* tour started out with a pair of appearances in Germany before the band returned to the States for what would be a truncated series of US shows in Los Angeles, California, Amherst, New York and Somerset, Wisconsin. America continued to be an uphill battle. Starting afresh with a new American label, and with *Fully Completely* receiving only lukewarm reviews and miniscule amounts of airplay, The Hip were essentially at square one, with the band usually finding themselves playing small venues and, in many cases, largely to audiences of ex-patriots and loyal Canadians who had made the trek across the border to support their native sons.

From The Tragically Hip's inception, the band always encouraged their fans to have a good time at their concerts and to express themselves just about any way they wanted. But they were realists when it came to their own personal safety. The Amherst show would be a prime example. Things were going well until a fan decided to fling a shoe at the band. The shoe struck Downie in the head. The band walked off the stage, effectively ending their show. And in the overall scheme of things, who could blame them?

After a quick side trip to The Netherlands, the band returned to Canada and the start of what would be four all-day festivals under the Another Roadside Attraction banner. The vibe at these shows was communal, almost Woodstock-like in an obviously scaled down manner. But as the first show commenced, there was some tension between Midnight Oil and The Hip. There was some concern that fans would disrupt Midnight Oil's set with cries of "Hip Hip". But it would turn out that Hip fans could be respectful in the face of the legendary Australian band and did not start chanting for The Hip until Midnight Oil had finished their set.

Another possible source of friction was the ingrained sense of competitiveness between the two bands. Sinclair recalled in the book *Have Not Been the Same* that some nights respect and fear went hand in hand. "The first couple of shows, going on after Midnight Oil, was the hardest thing we'd ever had to do. The overall quality of the music was amazing. The Oils were so intense and so good, musically, but you know they were out to steal the audience every night. You knew they wanted to take us down every night and they played like it."

While the band had always been available to play for worthy local charities and fundraisers, being on the road with Midnight Oil, who had always been out front in political and social issues, turned out to be a formative period. Shortly after the conclusion of the Another Roadside Attraction shows, The Hip participated in a day long Kumbaya Festival for AIDS research. But by that time, Midnight Oil had already given them a real-world taste of how music and philanthropy could mix.

Environmental causes were a hallmark of Midnight Oil's agenda and, as the Another Roadside Attraction shows continued, The Tragically Hip had a front row seat on Midnight Oil's participatory nature. Protest had been growing in Canada over the cutting of old growth forest at Clayquot Island, and Midnight Oil would be quick to jump into the protest, showing up and playing an impromptu set on the site of a logging road blockade. But that was not the end of the defiance. When it was suggested that a protest single to raise money for the cause was a sound idea, the song "Land" was born in an impromptu recording session that had the singers of all the bands currently on the tour, including Downie, contributing a verse. The experience of being involved in Midnight Oil's political and environmental stance was not lost on The Hip. Sinclair, in a quote that appeared in the book *Have Not Been the Same: The CanRock Renaissance*, explained how Oil taught his band quite a bit about the power of music.

"We really got a sense of what the power of music was all about, especially from The Oils. We really learned a lot from those guys about the message you're getting across. We went from being this little barroom band to being more grown up by the end of the tour."

Typical of the way The Tragically Hip worked, the tour in support of *Fully Completely* also saw the band workshopping new material in the live setting. Two songs of note were a tough love and relationship tune called "Thugs" and a song that literally came to life during a series of free form jams called "Nautical Disaster." Both songs were destined to wind up on their next album.

In the meantime, the struggles with *Fully Completely's* attempts to crash the long elusive US market continued. The album would fail to chart in America, as would follow up singles "At the Hundredth Meridian" and "Looking for a Place to Happen." But, as always, in Canada The Tragically Hip could do no wrong. The reviews were ecstatic in their praise and there was excited speculation at the potential of the band heading off in a new direction.

And in their follow up album, *Day for Night* (the title taken from the Francois Truffaut art film of the same name), that new direction would be dark, moody and introspective. Why The Hip would go in what appeared to be a very non-commercial and, to fans and critics alike, very contrary direction to *Fully Completely* is open to conjecture. Some speculated that it was road weariness that had inspired the change while others offered that the continued failure to spread the band across their firewall of Canada and into the States had given them a bad case of the pissed off's. In any case, *Day for Night* would be a surprise.

And in many cases a surprise to the band. Whether or not a conscious decision, The Tragically Hip's musical plans for the album, which would be recorded in Kingsway Studio (New Orleans) and Le Cave de Dave (Kingston, Ontario) would by design move away from the blues-rock stylings of previous albums and into a realm of stark and anthemic. The story and the lyrics were even more to the fore. *Day for Night* still showcased The Tragically Hip as a rock and roll band but, by degrees, it also showcased the band deep in shadows. A *Windsor Star* reporter questioned Downie about the musical changes in *Day for Night* and the singer seemed stumped for an answer. "I don't think you can ever really plan changes beforehand," he said. "If you work hard enough, I don't think it's possible to just repeat what you're doing."

The Hip quickly recruited producer Mark Howard and longtime friend and front of the house travelling sound engineer Mark Vreeken to produce the album. And for the first time, The Tragically Hip would take a producer's credit, justifying the move by stating that they knew what they wanted and how they wanted it done. Demos would be recorded and songs eventually paired down.

However, according to Howard's comments in a *Hamilton Spectator* interview, he saw the big challenge in *Day for Night* to be the changing around of the band's overall sound. "I thought they needed a new sound sonically," he related. "They've been slightly uninteresting for the past while but, this time, I was into having the band take some chances."

And those changes were often difficult for the band. The intent, unlike the conventions in play on *Road Apples*, were extremely down played and under produced. Stripped of all but the bare musical essentials, the songs on *Day for Night* were allowed to breathe. "They were nervous about some of the guitar and drum techniques I was asking for," related Howard. "But what I was trying for was to create more of a deeper image than simply guitars in your face."

The *Day for Night* sessions were a restless time for The Hip. Personally, members of the band were growing up and embarking on the road to relationships and marriages which could not help but impact their professional lives.

Finding any but the most fragmentary information about the band members' families proved next to impossible as the members of the band had always been extremely private when it came to their private lives and spouses. One advantage in the musicians settling down when they did was that they were fairly well-established by the time they began having serious relationships and marriages. Consequently Hip wives were entering a situation that was, financially and otherwise (by rock and roll standards) fairly safe and comfortable.

Laura Leigh Usher (Downie's wife) reportedly worked in the real estate industry while Kathryn Humphreys (Fay's wife) worked for a number of years as an on Air Canadian television sports reporter for City TV. Joanne Langlois (Langlois' wife) is a clothing designer and involved in many charitable causes and Leslie Galbraith (Baker's wife) is active on the social and arts scene. It would be at the last possible moment before going to the publisher that a series of emails disclosed that Gord Sinclair had not only been married to Christene Sinclair but that they had subsequently divorced at an undisclosed date.

But one can easily surmise that the members of The Hip had survived the rigors of groupies and failed relationships to have finally found their soulmates. To form permanent bonds with the members of the band, and fairly long-lasting ones at that, it is a safe bet that all were, to an extent, all politically and socially aware, well-educated and in line with varying degrees of activism. But easily the most telling aspect of their relationships had to be their ability to marry into the rock and roll lifestyle that The Tragically Hip lived and breathed.

With the band constantly either on the road or in the recording studio, all the women in their lives most likely played both the mother and father roles to their children while their men were away. Trust may well have been one of their strongest traits when it came to Hip wives. Trust, and lest we forget, love.

For Fay and Humphreys, the challenges were many. Their respective jobs often have kept them apart for long periods of time. It was also a six-year struggle with infertility that put added pressure on the relationship. But Fay and Humphreys persisted and the couple were finally blessed with twins. Of the occasion, Humphreys offered in pre-delivery bliss, "Johnny and I are over the moon."

Day for Night had evolved into something resembling a personal and creative crusade, one that, at every turn, was flying in the face of everything, musically that had gotten them to this point. There was a lot of musical energy abroad in these sessions and it would result in too much energy for just one album.

Enter *The Shadow Album*.

Information on this 'mystery disc' is admittedly

slim. Almost all of which was supplied by producer Howard in an interview with *The Hamilton Spectator*. "It's called *The Shadow Album.* A couple of things on it are pretty outside. This is more of a film soundtrack stylish work." Howard acknowledged that this album was completed but that he had no idea if it would be released in the future. Although one observer, who asked that his name not be used, did speculate that some of that mystery material might have sneaked into small moments during the band's live shows of that day.

In its own way, *Day for Night*, in the period leading up to its September 24, 1994 release was a mystery as well, and from a purely bottom line business sense, a fairly scary proposition at that. Word of how dark the album actually was proved an understatement. From first cut to last, *Day for Night* was downright terrifying, its dense mental sense of introversion and hopelessness was striking a tone that was perceived as even causing loyal Canadian fans pause to shudder. And singles? In the classic sense, there truly was not any, with only "Thugs" and "Fire in the Hole" coming remotely close. In many corporate circles, the album was quietly being considered DOA.

But upon its release, *Day for Night* seemingly had the gods on its side.

The album would sell 300,000 copies within four days of its release and would quickly make it to No. 1 on the Canadian chart. While the reviews were decidedly mixed, with words such as 'lackluster' and 'dark' being freely tossed around, loyal fans seemed to get it or, at least, want to. The first single off *Day for Night*, "Grace, Too," jumped high onto the Canadian charts and would ultimately peak at No. 11. The follow up single, "Greasy Jungle" would make it to No. 8 but that essentially chewed up any commercial capital the album might have had. Four more singles, "Nautical Disaster" (No. 26), "So Hard Done By" (No. 64), "Scared" (No. 57) and, almost as an afterthought "Thugs" which would limp in at No. 81, had hit the proverbial brick wall as far as Canadian radio acceptance went. The consensus being that dark and downer Tragically Hip, despite the fact that *Day for Night* would ultimately register at six times platinum, was, in the long run, not easily digestible.

But even an uneven acceptance in The Hip's home country was positively rapturous when compared to the across the board goose eggs that the band registered on both the US album and singles' charts.

When it came to *Day for Night*, America did not know the album had ever existed.

Chapter Ten
Playing with the Big Boys

One week after the release of *Day for Night* and The Tragically Hip were already back on the road. It was a tour that would consist of largely US dates and the irony was that their sets were consisting largely of songs from *Day for Night*, the record that US markets would choose to ignore. Which, as a piece in *Canoe Jam.com* would reveal, was pretty much par for the course.

The story indicated that the relationship with US label Atlantic Records had been largely hit or miss. Tours were thrown together, seemingly, in a haphazard manner and there had never been a definitive marketing plan to break The Hip in the United States. But the band remained determined and, with the exception of a week's worth of shows in Europe, the group's schedule was confined to the States, largely medium-sized club gigs, with no Canadian shows on the itinerary. But once it became evident that their music remained largely a mystery in the States, the band returned north of the border and to the place where they were considered stars.

And, early in '95, the band continued to thrive on

home cooking. In February, The Hip sold out their Pacific Coliseum show in 20 minutes. It was not long after that show that fate increased their audience size to 18 million.

Saturday Night Live alum and occasional guest host Dan Aykroyd had long been an avid fan of The Tragically Hip. So much so that, when he accepted a hosting gig on an upcoming episode of *SNL*, he insisted that The Hip be the show's musical guest. The band accepted the opportunity to finally get in the collective faces of US music lovers. But it would be done their way. With so many albums and songs in their catalogue, it seemed logical for the band to play one or two of their greatest hits. But, when Aykroyd introduced the band on March 25, 1995, he was probably shocked when The Hip immediately broke into "Nautical Disaster" and "Grace, Too," songs from the almost unknown (to US audiences) *Day for Night*.

Live television was totally alien turf for the band but, in hindsight, they made it work. Downie, in conversations with *The Georgia Straight* and *The Hamilton Spectator*, talked about the experience in terms of its unexpected intimacy. "We did reach a much wider audience with *Saturday Night Live*. The *Saturday Night Live* thing, on a personal level, was easily the most intimate gig we've ever done. You're looking at this camera and all of a sudden less becomes more. It was quite an experience. The camera made it an intimate experience. It instantly became a one-on-one experience and, with the camera, the smallest gestures can say so much."

The *Saturday Night Live* appearance would kick off a mammoth summer tour, easily one of their most ambitious to date, that would take The Hip through countless shows in Canada, America and Europe. It was also a concert tour that would be highlighted by an unexpected phone call...

...From singer Robert Plant with an offer The Tragically Hip could not refuse. Plant and his former mate from Led Zeppelin, guitarist Jimmy Page, were about to embark on a North American tour and were looking for an opening act. Sinclair, in the book *Has Not Been the Same: The CanRock Renaissance*, recalled the moment.

"I didn't know whether it was a good idea for us, commercially to support them. But when Robert Plant phones you up and asks if you want to do it, what are you supposed to say? It was the opportunity of a lifetime."

The Tragically Hip made their debut on the Page and Plant tour on May 1. And, despite their years on the road, they knew immediately that they had suddenly found themselves in the rarified atmosphere of rock royalty. The Led Zeppelin vibe was everywhere. Everything seemed larger than life and quite above it all. But The Hip seemed to adjust very quickly. Page and Plant were accommodating, welcoming and quite the rock and roll hosts.

As for the guys in The Tragically Hip? They quickly settled into yet another road routine. Before the shows, the Canadians would usually find the time to indulge their hockey aesthetic by organizing loose roller hockey games in a venue parking lot, which often found their frustrated road manager having to track them down and herd them onto the stage with literally minutes to spare.

Not surprisingly, the band, as opening act, was not afforded a whole lot of stage time. Also not surprising was that Downie, in assessing the Page and Plant experience in *The Hamilton Spectator* and *The Georgia Straight*, came down on both the ying and yang of it all. "I liked it and I didn't like it. With Page and Plant, we did 30 minutes a night and that, practically speaking, is just not enough time. Forty-five minutes to me is the optimum, anything less than that is a real physical challenge. I was stunned and baffled, just because of the actual experience of doing it. As far as playing to their crowd, that was neat. We had never really done that before and I think we needed to do it."

The Page and Plant tour chugged along through the end of May like a well-oiled machine. Opening for and then watching two of the greatest rock talents of the modern era perform on a nightly basis was a psychological rush and education. Downie saw it as a kind of Zen/Star Wars experience in conversation with *The Hamilton Spectator*. "It was very fateful somehow. It was like some Jedi Master somewhere had decided that we needed this as the next stage in our education."

The second phase of The Tragically Hip's rock star wet dream would come in early June when the call came that The Rolling Stones were interested in having the band open for them in a series of four shows in Europe. The Page and Plant tour had always been a fluid situation and The Hip were allowed to temporarily work around breaks in P & P's schedule and jump ship to open for The Stones.

Opening for The Rolling Stones struck a

particularly nostalgic tone with the band. A decade earlier the then very young and virginal Tragically Hip would sit around for hours in Baker's basement, struggling to pick out the chords to the most obscure Stone's songs they could find. And it was with those memories still strong in their minds that The Hip stood offstage, waiting to go on for the first time in front of a literal tidal wave of rabid Stones' fans.

"We were nervously swaying back and forth and breathing deeply and about to go on in front of 72,000 Stones' fans," Downie recalled in a *The Georgia Straight* story that was heavy on psychology. "We're a necessary function [to the show]. They can't really get by without you but, at the same time, it's tough. You go up and play 30 or 45 minutes and you feel a bit stunted and a bit restrained. Which is something I, personally, am not used to dealing with."

But the exposure certainly did not hurt and the result was that the band returned to the States creatively recharged and ready to kick off what was shaping up as a semiannual event, the Another Roadside Attraction festival series. By now thoroughly entrenched in the idea of using the shows to raise money for various international charities. The Hip continued to be extremely hands on when selecting the bands that would perform at these festivals, often spending hours at a time brainstorming who they felt would make the best possible support show. The Hip chose wisely, collecting a core group that included Rheostatics, Mathew Sweet, Spirit of The West, Ziggy Marley and Blues Traveler while adding one shot supporting acts along the way.

"It's a fun project for us," Downie enthused to

The Hamilton Spectator. "It's sort of a dream job for us. You're able to phone up musicians and say, 'You may not have heard of us, but we definitely like you and we'd love you to come play with us in Canada."

Following the conclusion of the Another Roadside Attraction shows, The Hip barely took a breath before jumping back on the road with solo shows in both the US and Canada as well as continuing as support group for the remainder of the Page and Plant American dates. With one more break that nobody could reasonably argue with.

The Hip had to cancel a week's worth of P and P dates between October 12 and 17 when Langlois' wife, Joanne, went into labor and the couple's first child was born. On October 18, the band returned to the Page and Plant tour. The only discernible difference was that Langlois just could not stop smiling.

The Page and Plant tour concluded at the end of October. The Hip would carry on for another three weeks before finally packing in one of their most memorable tours to date. As always, it would be up to Downie to put what had transpired in the proceeding months in its proper perspective.

"There must have been some kind of fateful activity at work here," he told *The Georgia Straight*. "It must be some kind of message."

'

Chapter Eleven
Hip in the Hen House

The Hip's Langlois can be nothing if not candid. While Downie, Baker, Sinclair and, on rare occasion, Fay have always been highly quotable, Langlois has rarely proven more than a stealth quote. But all of that suddenly changed in 1996 when, in conversation with *Drop D Magazine*, he matter-of-factly gave up the ghost. The ghost in The Tragically Hip's case being that the band had long ago given up the idea of being superstars in America.

"The chance of us breaking the States is probably decreasing," he said. "I think we would be shocked if it happened. We've never really expected to do that. If we did break that market, I think that we would have a sense that it would be a strain on our personal lives."

Much of Langlois' downplaying of the importance of US success could easily be traced to the fact that they had grown comfortable with their lot in life. Their albums and singles regularly charted high in Canada and their tours in their home country typically sold out in the thousands, in stark contrast to the fact that their records, quite simply, did not chart in America and their tours south of the border were primarily clubs whose capacity never rose above 800.

They were Gods in Canada. They were "Tragically who?" in the States. The band was beginning to take the hint as well as taking the bull by the horns

The Tragically Hip had been the students at the feet of a number of producers. They had learned a lot but, by the time they had completed *Day for Night*, they were chaffing at the idea of having the band ideas filtered through a non-band party, with Langlois, diplomatically, offering in *Drop D* that, "There was some give and take with producer Mark Howard." Add to that the fact that the band had spent the better part of a year on the road and were pretty much burned out and you had a recipe for the band pulling inward for their next album.

The Tragically Hip decided that it was time to produce themselves, with a little help from long time Hip live sound and studio engineer Mark Vreeken. Downie acknowledged in the *Tucson Weekly* that having a steady hand around was important to the band's maiden production. "We were concerned about taking that leap without having the sort of nurse, nanny, father figure, psychologists, field general around.

The band also felt that from a pure comfort level, it would be wise to record close to home. Hence, The Bathouse Studio, long owned and operated by the band and located just outside of Kingston, proved the ideal place. "We always wanted our own studio, somewhere we could leave our gear and jam and record some stuff when we wanted, Langlois told *Drop D*. "That was always one of our goals."

For the band, the goal of *Trouble at the Henhouse* was to make music in a freewheeling manner, mixing and matching the band's tried and true musical and lyrical experiments, including equal amounts of philosophy and

Canadiana as well as acoustic, psychedelic and just batty influences and unexpected turns. In other words, The Tragically Hip would be having fun and the result would be whatever it turned out to be.

There was a sense among observers that The Tragically Hip were due for a stopgap album, something that would reinforce the very elements that got The Hip to their current station and that would allow them to breath before setting their sights on the future. The band could not argue with that sentiment.

"We didn't make *Trouble at the Henhouse* for the fans," Langlois told *Drop D*. "That's no offense to the fans, but we made it for ourselves."

Trouble at the Henhouse sessions would be tentative. The Hip had their songs already to go. They had what could be singles in the songs "Gift Shop," "Ahead by a Century," "Springtime in Vienna" and "700 Foot Ceiling" but while the perception was that the songs were solid, prototypical Hip, none were perceived as world beaters. The vibe in the studio was, likewise, easygoing.

There would be disagreements on how certain songs should come across musically and lyrically but, sometimes, the solution was as easy as rearranging the instruments to different parts of the studio. For first time producers, the members of The Tragically Hip, aided by Vreeken, seemed to have a handle on how the album should come together. Time seemed to be a major factor. They had lots of it. The close proximity to their respective families made for a relaxed atmosphere. Downie put the vibe succinctly in a *Tucson Weekly* quote when he stated, "We think what you're hearing [on the album] is that deep low sigh of a band that's getting what it wanted.

The 'fun' aspect of the sessions was echoed by Sinclair when he recalled to *Hip Online.com* that "*Henhouse* for us was a lot of fun to make. We had bought the house and just made the record. We did not have anyone looking over our shoulders.

Trouble at the Henhouse was released on May 7, 1996. The response was mixed and often damning with faint praise. While there was a lot to like with the album, critics quickly picked up on the fact that *Trouble at the Henhouse* was largely going over old ground. In their eyes, this was an album that would, most certainly, satisfy the legions of fans but would not go far in expanding their audience. Given these dire predictions, *Trouble at the Henhouse* would do much better than expected

The biggest surprise was that the album managed to crack the US album chart. Granted, it would peak at No. 134 and disappear in a matter of weeks. But it was considered progress. In Canada it would be a decidedly different story. *Trouble at the Henhouse* would make it to No. 1 in record time and remain there for four weeks. The first single off the album, "Ahead by a Century," made it to No. 1 on the Canadian Singles chart and would ultimately be the first Tragically Hip single to be certified platinum. Follow up singles, "Gift Shop," "700 Ft. Ceiling" and "Springtime in Vienna," would also do reasonably well. *Trouble at the Henhouse* would finally do all around respectable business. But inside corporate walls, whispers could be heard that maybe, sales wise, The Tragically Hip had peaked.

'The Hip kicked off their '96 tour on a nostalgic note on May 6 with the first of two shows at The

Horseshoe Tavern. Then it was off for what would turn out to be their most extensive US tour to date with literally two months of crisscrossing America with occasional quick hops back into Canada along the way. The set list for those shows was, primarily, songs from *Trouble at the Henhouse* but, eventually, older Hip standards began to be added.

Midway through the '96 tour, The Tragically Hip decided that their upcoming show in Detroit would be the ideal show to record for a live album. It was a decision that left many observers scratching their heads. Cynics pointed to the band's decision as a sign that The Hip were burned out, creatively, and that live albums were what band's usually did when they were buying time or that they were looking to get out of a contract. As it would turn out, that assessment was partially true. Their deal with MCA in Canada was still strong. Atlantic on the other hand, had become frustrated with the stateside label's inability to break the band in America and, after *Trouble at the Henhouse*, had come to the conclusion that it was time to drop the band.

What passed for the official announcement from Atlantic was vague at best. "We went above and beyond promotionally with this band," said Atlantic Records VP Vicky Germaise. "But we were not able to surmount the boundaries that exist for them in this market."

Once again orphaned in America, The Hip were, doubtless, feeling the angst, anger and frustration; the anecdotes which, in the past, had translated to the band at their best on stage. The Cobo Hall show would prove the definitive chronicle of the band at their performing best. Downie was at his best that night, alternating a Jim Morrison style of banter before, during and after just about every song, incorporating, literally out of nowhere, lyrics from other people's songs and giving an education on how to be a rock and roll front man. Not that the remainder of The Hip were just slouches along for the ride. The combined sounds of guitar, bass and drum anchored both a fiery constant groove and moments of sheer individual bombast. If *Live Between Us* would be considered a throwaway upon its release, the album had some surprises in store. Because *Live Between Us* would be the perfect album to dissect by those searching for what made The Tragically Hip tick. And *Live Between Us*, all 70 odd minutes of it, would be a classic sonic textbook.

And while America, not surprisingly, was nowhere to be found on the charts, Canada was representing in a fairly big way. The week of *Live Between Us'* release, eight songs off the album made it into the Canadian Top 20 Singles chart. The album would go the equivalent of Canadian double platinum by August, selling more than 400,000 copies by the end of the year, while picking up significant sales in Europe.

Nineteen ninety-seven would test The Tragically Hip on a number of levels. While not completely giving up on making it big in America, the failure with Atlantic had now put the US way back in their list of priorities. In their minds, Canada would always be there and that fact alone meant a lot as Sinclair explained in *The Queens Journal*. "We're in a position where we can tour when we want to tour. We don't have to record until we're finished writing. We have the freedom to get together and be creative with each other for a living."

Chapter Twelve
Hip in a Hard Place

But were The Tragically Hip on the verge of losing their mojo? There were two sides to this story going into 1998. Quite simply, the diehard fans loved everything the band put out. But lurking in the critical caverns of the last two studio albums and the live album were decidedly mixed reviews that seemed to indicate that while The Hip could not be matched in a live setting, their studio sound had often seemed compromised by the emerging technology. Catch the always candid Hip in interview and there would be hints that they got the picture and were doing a lot of woodshedding in an attempt to bring their studio output up to the level of *Road Apples* and *Fully Completely*.

"This was the record we had to make at this juncture in our career," Downie told *Canadian Musician Magazine*. "We had the time to approach it with a 'no stone unturned' philosophy. We had the time to work on things and bring our ideas to fruition."

The first step on the road to *Phantom Power* was to stay at home. The band had loved the idea of recording at their Bathouse Studio on their previous studio album and it was clear that their next album would also be created there. And while they now felt confident around the recording studio, they felt a practiced hand turning the knobs would be the way to go.

They found what they needed in producer and Los Lobos musician Steve Berlin. Berlin, who had produced a number of Canadian acts during the early 90's, got up close and personal with The Tragically Hip when Los Lobos was asked to join the band during the 1997 Another Roadside Attraction series of shows. It did not start out as a de facto audition for Berlin and the band but, according to Berlin during a *Maclean's* conversation, from his point of view that's what it turned out to be.

"Watching them [The Hip] work every night on stage for a month and getting to know them all, that's when we became much closer."

Shortly after Another Roadside Attraction, Berlin was officially asked to ramrod the album that would be *Phantom Power*. "All the work they've done and what they represent culturally is unique," assessed Berlin. "Frankly, all of that was something I had to ignore in order to make a good album with them. I couldn't be worrying about tarnishing a legend."

Berlin's arrival came at a perceived turning point in The Tragically Hip's musical odyssey. After spending their entire career plowing the fields of pure and basic rock and roll energy, The Hip was moving forward and embracing abstraction and acoustic sensibilities. In their own way, the band was trending economically yet in a highly stylized and progressive way. And, by association, becoming a bit more pop oriented.

Berlin went into the *Phantom Power* sessions ready to move in any direction. There were no discussions with the band and the producer, most certainly, did not have a personal agenda. But he did relate in *Maclean's* that the band did have ideas. Lots of them. "They had sent me probably 30 tapes, not so much individual songs but ideas and riffs. There might have been 15 actual songs and 15 'things.' Their song "Poets" was a perfect example of how things tended to work. The chorus and solo parts were sent to me as three separate elements and I put them together. Some songs were ready and some had to tinker with a little. We had so many cool ideas to mess with."

During the sessions, Berlin was also witness to the sometimes goofy, sometimes real world emotions within the band. There were a lot of stories about their high school days. There were moments of dissension, arguing and fighting. The *Phantom Power* sessions brought out the asshole in everybody in the band at one point or another. For Berlin, his biggest struggles in the band would come when he would go toe to toe with Downie over seemingly insignificant questions.

"It was life or death. Every syllable was important. We would have silly, I wouldn't say arguments, but he would want me to push back on whether he should say 'a' or 'the' and which was the most powerful to say. It seemed silly but it mattered to him."

The result of all the low-key turmoil was that *Phantom Power* resulted in some solid Hip songs, stepped in history, known and obscure, raw emotion and an increased sense, even by Hip standards, of musical time and space. "Bobcaygeon," which would ultimately be hailed as one of The Tragically Hip's most endearing songs, referenced the Christie Pits riot of 1933 in which anti-Semitic thugs clashed with working class Toronto Jewish immigrants. "Escape Is The Hand of the Travelin' Man" would prove a taut and melancholy slice of obscure pop history as it chronicled the life of a Midwest pop/punk band named Material Issue and the mysterious suicide of one of its members, Jim Ellison.

The Tragically Hip and Material Issue had crossed paths during a long, arduous US tour. Downie and Ellison reportedly hit it off. Baker talked about the broader inspiration for the song in a conversation reported by *Hip fans.com*. "You meet these people that are exactly in the same boat and you have a natural kinship. You say, 'Oh man, we gotta get together.' You really hit it off and then at the end of the night, you go your separate ways, continue to do your thing and probably never see them again. It's strange but it's quite a common event, meeting people that you feel like you've known all your life, and then you really know them for half an hour."

Another song, "Something On," reportedly was created from whole cloth in the studio when the biggest ice storm in the history of the region settled in and the band were locked in with nothing else to do but create music. In any case, the reports of the music coming out of the *Phantom Power* sessions were reportedly a decided mix of quirky and conventional, drawing from The Tragically Hip's perceived strengths and showcasing their willingness to try something different.

The first indication that The Hip were onto something came in June when the first single off the album, "Poets" was released. The radio friendly song would immediately find its way to No. 1 on Canada's Alternative Singles charts and stay there for an unprecedented 12 weeks. *Phantom Power* would be released in July with an unveiling at their old performing haunt, The Horseshoe Tavern. The album would debut at No. 1 on the Canadian Album charts, selling an unprecedented 108,000 copies, literally in a day.

Phantom Power would make a token appearance on the US album charts at No. 143 and follow up singles in Canada ("Fireworks" No. 9 and "Bobcaygeon" No. 3). But, finally, *Phantom Power* would be one of those Tragically Hip albums that would have fans and critics choosing up sides. Fans being fans thought the album was a daring and largely self- indulgent, yet successful, next step. Collectively scratching their heads, critics gave *Phantom Power* a mixed review, alternately insightful and just as often maybe a bit too out there for its own good. But all would acknowledge that The Hip had taken an important development step in their ability to, quite naturally, flip musical styles with both ease and daring and that Downie's storytelling skills were spot on, addressing the band's Canadian sense while taking new steps into a lyrical world that would seemingly continue to take flight.

But the true lessons within the band would truly be learned during the band's 1998 *Phantom Power* tour, deep, thoughtful questions about The Hip having reached that magic plateau where fans quite literally hung on every word, acted out in rock concert clichés that were often in contrast to the values and attitudes of the band themselves.

The tour would be a six month long monster beginning in Canada before a long trek through the United States (where despite continued lax commercial acceptance, The Hip's live shows had grown) and then back to Canada for an end of the year wrap up. Much of the live experience, sprinkled with expected surprises, had pretty much become rote. But then there was the July 7 show in London, Ontario.

From the outset, the crowd was enthusiastic and prone to aggressive rounds of crowd surfing. It was a practice that Downie found annoying and downright dangerous. One hour into the Hip set, the show was suddenly stopped when an audience member fell to the ground during crowd surfing and the show had to be stopped while he was attended to. Whether it was a band decision or, more likely, Downie's, the band arbitrarily cut their set short and left the stage. At one point before the stoppage, Downie yelled at the crowd, "Crowd surfing went out with acid wash! Don't go there!"

The tour would occasionally highlight the often exhausting schedule the band had set for themselves. During an acoustic set in Sausalito, California, Downie had a mid-song brain freeze when he suddenly was unable to hit the high notes on the song "Thompson Girl" and, in a fit of frustration, stopped singing. The rest of the band barely blinked an eye when they finished the rest of the song while Downie remained mute.

With the tour came the inevitable pre and post show interviews with the local press and rock radio personalities. The Hip would usually designate one or two members with that chore and would be professional and courteous when they were seemingly dealing with the same, very tired questions at every stop. During their Redmond, Washington stop, Baker and Downie were being interviewed by the local radio personality who, it became evident, had not really done his homework, repeatedly asking the band about their lack of US success. Baker bit his tongue and dutifully answered the pat questions with the pat answers. He was a lot more accommodating than Downie who had a sour look on his face as he sat quietly, saying nothing. Downie would later acknowledge that he had been disappointed that people were still beating the lack of US success questions to death.

Playing the Grape Jam Music Festival in Pennsylvania was also a shining example of how Downie could be a bit of a drama queen even while couching it in concern for his fans. During their set, fans near the front of the stage were constantly pushing and shoving each other with only a flimsy snow fence separating the throng from the stage. Downie would repeatedly plead with the fans to stop the hijinks before somebody got hurt. Downie would finally have enough when the fence gave way and dozens of people fell on top of each other. The band left the stage without finishing the set.

Downie once quipped in a *CBC music.com* conversation about his concern for fan safety, "Be safe. Have fun, live a long life and rock with The Hip."

Of the latter, fans most certainly did. The '98 tour was, in hindsight, considered a celebratory party, a coming out and legitimizing of the band's status as full-blown stars in Canada. It was a tour that was never at a loss of surprises that would test the band's sense and sensibilities. Case in point being the band's show in New Hampshire when, midway through the song "Hard Done By," a woman suddenly jumped on stage and began to dance. Downie was reportedly so surprised that he forgot the next verse of the song. But ever the good sport, when security attempted to take the woman off the stage, he waved them off and let her stay. He would later introduce the woman to the crowd by saying, "This is Heather from The Jimmy Buffett Band."

Although The Tragically Hip's set was fairly pat with certain songs always being played for maximum audience impact, the band would always seem to showcase those fluid moments and bring long abandoned songs out into the light. One such instance at a Washington DC, The Hip dragged the song "On the Verge," a song they had not played live in five years, out for a spirited blow. A week later in New York, the band unveiled the song "Boots or Hearts" for a live go for the first time in seven years.

They also shook up the tour and the perception of the band by playing second fiddle at several multi band outdoor festivals and serving as opening act for both Blues Traveler and Bruce Hornsby.

The Hip's and, seemingly Downie's, sensitivity toward the safety of his fans was being tested at nearly every turn as The Hip walked a fine line between audience enthusiasm and the concern for their health. The dichotomy was once again tested during an Albany, New York show when, midway through the first encore, an audience member tried to jump on stage, missed his landing and landed on the floor. Downie looked out over the lip of the stage, saw the fan lying motionless on the floor and, immediately, stopped the show, telling the audience as they walked off, "That I didn't want to stay and witness the carnage."

When things were good on The Hip's *Phantom Power* tour, they were spectacular. But every once in a while there was something looming in the wings to put them in their place. Exhibit A, The 40 Watt Club, a medium sized club in Athens, Georgia. On a good night, The 40 Watt Club could pack in 800 rockers. A good night was not what it was when The Tragically Hip rolled into town. Ticket sales for The Hip show had been extremely slow. There had been some grumbling that the show might be cancelled because of slow ticket sales. But the band were nothing if not troopers and had a history of playing some of their most memorable shows in front of crowds that numbered in the low double digits. So on November 2, 1998, 150 people hooted and hollered their way through a great set by the band.

The show at The 40 Watt Club would be the least attended on the *Phantom Power* tour. But it would be the most rocking show Athens, Georgia had seen in many a moon.

Chapter Thirteen
By the Time Hip Got to Woodstock

That The Tragically Hip had evolved into a juggernaut of a touring and recording band had been chalked up to youth, hunger and reality. They had to be out among them in order to have a career. But in a conversation with *Hip Online.com*, Sinclair pared the equation down to something a lot more basic and human. "I think we just get restless and bored of being on the road," he said. "So we go write and record. Then we get bored of being in the studio and want to get out and play in front of people."

As it would turn out, boredom from the road had not yet set in and, after a short break to be with family for the holidays, The Hip were back on the road January 29, 1999. The band, at this point, was, by degrees, attempting to inject a bit of stagecraft into their normal, threadbare, rock and roll presence. For a week before going back on the road, the band spent days crafting a more theater style setting to their live performance, complete with an ornate chandelier hovering over them. The first few weeks of this portion of the tour were rife with surprises as well as a bit of nostalgia. For the first time in many years, the band decided to revisit Charlotte

Town in Prince Edward Island. The band had always been playful in designing set lists that always seemed to be changing and, early in the tour, they surprised many when they decided, one night, to drop in a cover, *Save the Planet* by The Inbreds, into the mix. The Tragically Hip always seemed to be writing and working on new material and the road continued to be the place to woodshed, two examples being the in progress workouts on "Lofty Pines Motel" and "Never Ending Present."

Playing in Canada seemed the rock and roll equivalent of playing with house money. Critics who cast shade on a Tragically Hip performance did so at their own peril. But one early Canadian show would result in one critic casting stones when he dismissed a performance 'that contained too many slow songs' and the impression that 'the band wasn't really into it that night'. But the band brushed aside the critical barb as they moved across the border into the US.

The lack of any American commercial success did not seem to concern the band at this point. They were playing to progressively larger audiences in bigger and bigger venues. And while the Canadian contingent always followed and was ever present, US audiences were growing and catching The Tragically Hip vibe.

But the US portion of the tour would occasionally highlight the band's frustration of the perceived rock and roll lifestyle. The Hip had long established themselves as pure musicians dedicated to music as rock and roll art, predicated on the power of the song as a recording and in a live setting. They had little patience with the often media driven rock and roll lifestyle that often proved, at least to the band, a distraction. Especially to Downie.

The Grand Rapids, Michigan show would prove a case in point. Too much moshing and too much crowd surfing had driven the band's front man to near distraction. It seemed that Downie spent easily half the show expressing his displeasure at the antics to the audience to no avail.

And then there was Woodstock '99, a cynical and money driven attempt to recapture the spirit of the original Woodstock Festival 30 years later. Woodstock '99 would ultimately sink in a quagmire of poor planning, overpriced food and water and numerous reports of sexual assault. This would turn out to not be your parent's Woodstock and The Tragically Hip, early in the morning on opening day, were not immune from the harsh vibe circulating through the crowd. At one point in their set, the band attempted to generate some Canadian fervor by playing "Oh Canada" and was promptly shouted down by shouts of derision as well as a fusillade of rocks and bottles.

Some years later, Downie, in an introspective sit down with *No Depression*, would address the notion of celebrity and how fans react to the notion of their heroes as something to both aspire to and to serve them and their needs. "There is this popularity," he said. "Beer plus backward baseball caps plus obvious patriotic button pushing equals mass success. Well come on! Is that all there is?"

Following the Woodstock '99 show, the band returned to Canada for a couple of months of R&R. But while The Hip were spending quality time with their families, they never seemed far from each other and creative business. There would be moments when inspiration struck and the band members could be spotted going in and out of rehearsal space, playing with ideas that were resulting in a myriad of songs to be created and considered. There was also some very serious, albeit 'out there' notions being considered about the possibility of recording their next album while travelling the country on a train in deference to a 'back to the land vibe' that seemed to be permeating The Hip's psyche. It was safe to say that The Tragically Hip, now having arrived at a comfortable level of celebrity, were now more reflective and, perhaps, a tad spiritual in their outlook. The *Phantom Power* album and subsequent tour, had, creatively, gotten their minds right and was setting them down the road of change.

The Hip went back on a brief, two-stop in Toronto to end the year. Again, there was the good time vibe of being home among kindred and literal friends and it showed in two exemplary shows in which the band played much of the songs that got them there while tossing in a tantalizing hint or two of what might be around the corner. The second show, a December 31 New Year's Eve concert to bring on 2000, carried with it a nostalgic feel. It was the first time they had played a New Year's Eve show since 1991. That's when they pretty much had to pay the bills.

Now they did the show because they wanted to.

Chapter Fourteen
Alone/Together

As 1999 morphed into 2000, it was more than apparent that The Tragically Hip were taking on the mantle of rock elder statesmen. The band members had settled into middle age quite gracefully and had, well below the radar, put down familial roots and begun having children.

What would become of a rough and tough rock and roll band willingly going into a more comfortable state of mind was anybody's guess.

Producer Berlin who, at that time, was, likewise, dealing with expanding families and other than career issues, "They were all dealing with family vs. career issues. In a sense it seemed like a break. They're going to work each day was a break from what, to a degree, must have seemed like break from raising their families and having that responsibility."

Eventually the sheer logistics and time constraints of recording the album that would be *Music@Work* had the band changing their mind about recording on a moving train and, instead, deciding to return to the familiar confines of their Bathouse Studio. They had also decided they could avoid a lot of creative tension by once again getting Steve Berlin to produce. But if there was one telling sign that things were about to change it was the fact that, for the first time, musicians outside the band were brought into the studio.

Singularly and collectively, the members of The Tragically Hip had mixed and mingled quite easily with fellow travelers in the music community and, instinctively, sensed that the music on *Music@Work* was heading in directions that might require a bit of an outside assist. Hence, the invitation for Kate Fenner, Bruce McCulloch, Leah Fay and, Chris B Hannah Georgas to join the recording party.

Preparation for *Music @ Work*'s music was also expanding sound wise. The rough-hewn blues-rock that had gotten The Hip to this point was no longer subject to adjuncts to the band's largely trademark sound. Some songs would require odd sound effects. Drum machines and different types of percussion were added to some songs. As with previous albums, *Music@Work* would have its moments of push back between The Hip and producer Berlin.

"They seem to really enjoy time in the studio, as opposed to being outside the studio and dealing with stuff," he told *Maclean's*. "Like any band, there's a comfort zone that's hard to escape. You kind of need someone to tell you that. You think it's your vocabulary, but it's a cocoon that's safe. There was a bit of push back from the guys. But it didn't last long."

Largely thanks to the moment in the session when the band sat down to assess the song "Fireworks." The band was set up in their respective corners of the home studio when Berlin suggested they try something different. He moved the entire band into the kitchen area of the studio where they would play what turned out to be some of the best takes of the entire session. "Just taking them out of their comfort space was revelatory," recalled Berlin. "It helped them grasp the idea of changing the paradigm of everything else on the album."

Those privy to the *Music @ Work* sessions most likely saw quite the adventurous and challenging Tragically Hip studio experience to date. If the finished product would be an indication, the band's plan was no plan. From the heavy sonic assault of the songs "The Bastard" and "Freak Turbulence" to the soothing, if to many, off balance putting ballad "Toronto #4" and the folk strains of "As I Wind Down the Pines," the group was seemingly offering a sampler of musical styles without a hint of premeditation. Throw in the constant nibbling at third world influences and you had an album that challenged the perception of who The Tragically Hip was as a band.

Adding to the often slap dash nature of *Music @ Work* was Downie's lyrics which, on this album, trended more neo-hippie and dark with only the occasional nod to Canadian/historical influences. Collectively, The Hip, were seemingly coming to grips with mortality and, in particular, the notion of family and parenthood as a driving force in their lives. The result would be particularly evident in the song "My Music @ Work" in which there is a decided sense of playfulness and just plain silly attitudes mixing and matching easily with Downie's patented sense of irony.

Music @ Work would be released on June 6,

2000. But well before its official unveiling, the band was mentally preparing itself for the myriad of responses that was sure to follow. The consensus was that the band had done exactly what it had wanted to do musically and that they had wandered down some highly satisfying roads in the process. But The Hip were nothing if not realists when putting themselves in the minds of the fans who had come to associate a certain degree of expectation when it came to their favorite band.

Sometime after the release of *Music @ Work*, Downie would describe the album to *CBC Music.com* by stating "It's a generally misunderstood album that you love just the same as your other records."

Reviews of the album would be decidedly mixed but. Generally, lined up behind Downie in his 'misunderstood' stance. Some gave backhanded applause for the band's attempt at trying new things but were quick to point out that the seeming indiscriminate mixture of music styles was wildly inconsistent and often distracting. Others acknowledged the inclusion of so many additional musicians as sometimes distracting and occasionally moments that diluted the impact of individual members of the band. Not surprisingly, critics were making the point that Music@Work may well have been the band's least commercial album to date.

This would ultimately be borne out by the fact that even commercial radio seemed to be running the other way. The first single, *My Music @ Work* peaked on the Canadian singles chart at a disappointing No. 47 while, not surprisingly, the song did not chart in the US. Three follow up singles, "Lake Fever," "The Completists" and "Freak Turbulence," did not make the Canadian charts at all. The band would find solace in the fact that the album would go to No. 1 in Canada for a while and would actually chart in the US, albeit at a disappointing No. 139.

But Hip fans would remain loyal. *Music @ Work* would ultimately go twice platinum in Canada. Despite those continued solid sales, there were those bean counters who pointed out that sales for the album were noticeably down from those of its predecessor, *Phantom Power* which, in turn, had shown a sharp decline from *Trouble at the Hen House*.

By this time the band had found that the perfect elixir for bad news was to take their show on the road. And so, beginning mere days before the release of *Music @ Work* and lasting through the rest of the year, The Tragically Hip was on the road. The tour would be vintage Hip, a deft mixture of new and old songs with the generous amount of *Music @ Work* material proving a lot more powerful and enticing live than on record. Throughout US and Canadian shows, The Hip were in their element, away from the studio confines and inherent limitations, the band was stripped to its essence, musicians casting aside all but their basest and most powerful emotions and a singer whose lyrical heart was worn on his sleeve.

While outwardly, The Hip seemed comfortable in their place as rock's, at least in Canada, leading light and reigning superstars, privately there was, most certainly, something in the air. One could sense a yearning, always subtle but definitely there, that indicated that, collectively and individually, The Tragically Hip was looking for something more.

Which was, among other things, more family

time. But, as Sinclair would explain in a *Canoe Jam.com* conversation, The Hip, creatively, just needed some time apart to do their own thing. "Five guys writing songs together for years and years, you just get a backlog of material, some of which suggests other directions."

The band decided that the best course of action was to go off the road, for the better part of a year and change as it would turn out, and, in the best possible way, be apart for a while. Sinclair must have sensed that the inevitable rumors of the band breaking up would most certainly follow when he sat down to explain things with *Canoe Jam.com*. "I think the time apart was a great thing for Gord and a great thing for the rest of the band. We all got a chance to move off into other directions and Gord got a chance to explore. I think that anything like that is a positive and that it could only help all of us."

Sinclair's emphasis on Downie was the result of the singer/songwriter's internal struggles. Downie was legendary for carrying a notebook and pen with him wherever he went and often frantic when inspiration struck and he needed to get something down. More often than not, he would be satisfied and that what he had brought out of his psyche seemed to magically mesh with the rest of the band.

But by the time The Hip had completed *Music @ Work*, Downie was verging on a lyrical meltdown. "I just felt like trying something else," a candid Downie told *The Globe & Mail*. "I wanted a more measured connection with my craft. The writing I was doing was getting a little cold. I just needed more intimacy in the process."

To the extent that Downie became a creature of

the night as he cobbled together a series of fragments of old and, in some cases, forgotten songs from his creative back pages. After spending much of these days being a family man, Downie would go off to a private room around 10:00 p.m. each night, after his family had gone to sleep, and would turn inward as he turned out complete songs and poetry that would fit his eclectic vision. On a good night, Downie would accomplish enough to justify going to bed at 2:00 a.m.

"Some of them go way back," Downie told *Hiponline.com*. "I just started writing stuff in my book. I wanted to keep a diary. But I lacked the organizational skills so, at one point, I started disregarding the dates and just filling in the pages with stuff."

Ever the perfectionist, Downie found this seeming new foray into the literary world often become a trial by fire as he explained in *The Globe & Mail*. "I went to bed grumbling some nights, reluctant other nights. I would go over in my mind what constituted a good night or a bad night. I wouldn't know a seminal moment if it pissed on me but it became interesting because I never really thought about how to feed your head properly."

Whether by design or in a conscious attempt to make this just another Tragically Hip album, Downie decided the album would be created with non-Hip musicians. This created additional speculation that his solo effort would be testing the waters and that he might be getting ready to go it alone. But the band remained steadfast and supportive of what Downie would do and did not see the exclusion of them as a sign that the band was on the rocks.

Downie had made the acquaintance of countless

musicians over the years and literally had his pick of those willing to move heaven and earth to record with him. Downie's choices would be truly eclectic and off the beaten path, diverse talents Julie Doiron, Josh Finlayson. Atom Egoyan and members of the band The Dinner is Served who would form Downie's The Goddamned Band.

Irony in an old-school literary sense seemed to play a significant part in Downie's mental ramp up to the album that would be titled *Coke Machine Glow*. The Hip had their own studio in Kingston that would have served Downie's solo plans. However, the choice of a recording studio would ultimately land the singer/songwriter in Toronto where the long-standing DIY Gas Station Recording Studio, run by Downie compatriot and musician Dale Morningstar, had fallen victim to unsure economic times and corporate intrusion and was about to be torn down to make way for who knows what? Morningstar and others in the tiny complex were hanging on by a thread and were about to be evicted when Downie stepped in.

"Dale and all his neighbors were being ousted with very little notice so we would be the very last recording session before the wrecking ball hit," Down told *Hiponline.*

But while the specter of the studio literally being knocked down by a wrecking ball was a constant companion during the *Coke Machine Glow* sessions, the vibe, given the warm and intimate nature of the studio, was extremely relaxed and laidback. From the beginning, the live feel and a minimum of overdubs projected an 'of the moment' feeling to songs that ran the gamut from folk to lounge stylings. Downie was leaning heavily on the immediacy of the sessions, with the musicians hearing the songs and the music for the first time when they showed up to record and then were given only a couple of run throughs before the actual recording took place.

A total of eight songs were recorded that first day. A total of 16 songs, the entire length of the album, was reportedly in the can nine days later. That the songs play out in a smooth yet roughhewn way proved extraordinary by virtue of the fact that Downie had a literal open door policy during the recording in which a number of musicians literally walked in off the street, wanting to join the party and were allowed to contribute. Among those putting in bits and pieces were Travis Good (The Sadies), Kevin Hearn (The Barenaked Ladies) and Ron Sexsmith and Dave Clark (The Rheostatics).

Needless to say, Downie was thrilled with how such a seemingly unstructured and rag tag approach was working as he explained to *Hip Online*. "We were happy with the sounds we were getting and the sound of the room was very warm and intimate. There was a lot of preparation involved which made it easy to say 'let's do that' at the drop of a hat."

Downie pointed out in *Hiponline.com* that there was a deft mixture of taking the basic skeleton of a song and deciding the equation of musical addition or subtraction that makes it a good song. "Travis Good was amazing because if I needed a mandolin on one tune and a fiddle on another tune, all I have to do is wait for him to come in. Kevin Hearn on piano makes the song *Chancellor* the song it is. It was the same with Don Kerr, Julie [Dioron], Dale [Morningstar],

Josh [Finlayson] and Atom [Egoyan]. The song was there, people would come in and we would make things happen."

Coke Machine Glow was completed in May 2001 and would go out under the Weiner Art banner, a subsidiary label to The Hip's Universal Records. Initially, Downie had no plans to do any kind of tour behind the album but, perhaps more in homage to the simplicity of the album, decided on a mini tour of five shows, over a three-week period, hitting obscure places in the Canadian outback like Yellowknife and Guelph. Downie recalled in *Hiponline* that planning the mini tour was both amusing and enlightening. "I was thinking about going to Yellowknife because I had never been up there, actually none of us [his backup band] have been there and we were excited about traveling up there. The rest of the dates just seemed to flood in after Yellowknife. It was kind of like 'While you're out there, why don't you do this and this.' That's how playing in Guelph happened."

Playing those far flung dates with the inherent free time, what with traveling and all, continued to wet Downie's obsession with the writerly process. "I still had a longing interest in writing and continuing the process of writing every day. I started writing these poems and writing a book," he recalled to *Hiponline*. Word got around that Downie, having reworked the song lyrics of *Coke Machine Glow* into poetic form and adding new, original poems, had a completed book at hand. Vintage Canada (an imprint of Random House), one of the leading publishers north of the border, offered Downie a publishing deal for the manuscript and the idea of the book, initially, being released as a limited edition, companion element along with the album.

More than one observer looked askance at the notion of a cynical bit of cross marketing and the perception of Downie willingly going along with an uncharacteristic, for the singer, bit of name branding for the sake of a buck. Downie sidestepped the more cynical insinuations, hoping that if he was banking on celebrity, it would be in more satisfying directions. "I'd like to think that the franchising of my name only begins with the book," he candidly told *The Globe & Mail.* "But it probably began a long time ago."

Coke Machine Glow, the album and book were released in March 2001. The album and book would go their separate ways early in April. Both would be something that would have even the most ardent Hip/Downie fans choosing up sides and scratching their heads. On the up side, the album's seemingly modest intent was treated fairly, the occasional lyrical and instrumental flub more than salved by kudos for Downie's introspection, a lyrical aside to small, personal moments rather than the expected Canada centric moments that had permeated the Hip albums and the ease in which Downie had segued into something different. Critics were, on average, a bit more critical in many cases, stopping short of dismissing much of Downie's poetic efforts as disappointing or inconsistent.

Downie willingly did whatever press came his way and, happily, found a media that was happy to play to the literary side he was attempting with *Coke Machine Glow*. But Downie was realist enough to know going in that the commercial expectations for both the album and the book would be modest at best. But he had to be secretly pleased that *Coke Machine Glow* did manage to at least get on the Canadian album chart at No. 26.

But through it all, Downie remained philosophical and low key about his solo effort. As reported by *Jam Canoe.com* prior to the release of the album, Downie said, "I figure it will fulfill everyone's need. Those who needed to hate it would hate it and anyone who needed to love it would love it."

After the release of *Coke Machine Glow*, Downie maintained the same attitude. "I don't think anyone needs this record, period. No one needs any record or anything. I thought it would fulfill everyone's expectations...

..."And you know what? It has."

Chapter Fifteen
Blind Situation

Although *Coke Machine Glow* would ultimately satisfy Downie on a personal and creative level, the singer was never far from the question of what was next on the horizon for The Tragically Hip. On that front, Downie was quick to report to *Canoe.com* that the band was already doing much legwork for the next album. Albeit at a leisurely pace.

The band had been sending tapes of musical thoughts for some time to Downie, who, in turn, would factor in his own melodic and lyrical ideas before sending the tapes back to the band for further work.

"There's no real rush [about when we will record the next album], Downie told *Canoe.com*. "I will do my thing and the four of those guys are in Kingston. We are going to meet shortly. We make our decisions very slowly. The idea is that we will go into the studio when we know we have ten or 11 really good songs."

More as a lark than anything else, the band would get together as actors in the Canadian romantic comedy *Men with Brooms*, playing members of a hockey team in a cameo. The Hip would also contribute to the film's soundtrack with the song "Throwing Off Glass."

However, for many observers, the seemingly slow pace of gathering for the new album brought with it its own set of speculation. With the gradual decline in sales over the previous three albums, in particular in Canada, and the buzz surrounding Downie's solo effort, many feared that, creatively, the band had nothing new to say. Lyrically, it was a safe bet that Downie's more introspective turn, was forcing the remainder of the band to move even further away from their rock band roots and that some, if not all of the members, were allegedly having a tough time adjusting. But the reality was that much of the delay centered around The Hip pushing the envelope in terms of recording options.

First and foremost, after recording previous albums in the relative comfort of The Bathouse Studio, the band decided to move way off shore to The Bahamas' Compass Point Studios to record the album that would be entitled *In Violet Light*. Baker explained the reasoning behind the relocation in conversation with *Hiponline*.

"It was more a matter for us that Bath was so close to home," he said. "For me it's a twenty five minute commute, you work all day in the studio and then, at two o'clock in the morning, you have to drive home blurry eyed. Then in the morning, you have to wake up, make breakfast and get your son to school. I know it sounds incredibly selfish but all that outside stuff becomes a distraction. If we go away someplace where you just live and breathe the music, it just helps the band and we get a lot more quality work done in a short period of time.

Next on the album's to do list was to find a

producer. It had been discussed early on that going back to Steve Berlin might be the way to go. But the band sensed that they would need somebody new to compliment The Hip's newly evolving musical direction. In a conversation with *Canoe.com*, Sinclair recalled how they decided on Hugh Padgham.

"When we first started writing for the record, we realized that it was going to be like a live, compositional thing rather than a studio record. We put together a dream/wish list and Hugh was at or near the top of the list because of his work with Sting, The Police, David Bowie and XTC. We sent him the material and he got back to us right away. We jumped at the chance to work with him."

But, as explained by Baker in *Hiponline.com*, their enthusiasm was tempered by some reservations. Not the least of which is the fact that Padgham only had a nodding acquaintance with The Hip's sound and history.

"He had certainly heard of the band but I know he had never seen us live. To walk into a blind situation and let us give the project to him and say, 'You're in charge now.' I think it was strange and a bit of a leap of faith. But, as it turned out, he was a great choice for the band. He was interested in the atmosphere of the tune and the quickest way to build nice, tight and concise arrangements."

Despite his lack of familiarity of the band, Padgham acknowledged in a *Billboard* piece that one thing did immediately jumped out at him. "The current generation of American rock bands all sound the same. Given that, what's unique about The Tragically Hip is that they have a great sound."

Still, there was some lingering concern as The Hip

and Padgham convened in The Bahamas. To the public at large, the producer had made his bones with an often smooth, otherworldly tone, quite suited for the likes of The Police and Bowie. Would that approach work on The Tragically Hip, who were, at their core, your basic rock and roll band? But a rock and roll band that often fell prey to the eccentricities of Downie who, in *In Violet Light*, thought nothing of mixing influences, both forgotten and, thanks to his solo venture, newly discovered. In songs like "The Dire Wolf," "It's a Good Life if You Don't Weaken," "Silver Jet" and "The Darkest One," Downie seemingly roamed far afield and at the slightest whim, incorporating the influences of literary lights Wallace Stevens and Raymond Carver into tales both obscure and relevant, all seemingly wrapped up in economical, described by some as REM style punchy discourses in introspection, philosophical asides and wish fulfillment done up in songs that, surprisingly, were light on solos of any kind, yet musically taut in spirited arrangements.

Padgham knew what he was dealing with during the In Violet Light sessions. "I was determined to get the songs into as good a shape as possible," he told *Billboard*. "I was insistent we go through the arrangements and get them as succinct as we could."

Padgham's seen but not seen approach to producing found immediate favor with The Hip as Sinclair offered in *Billboard*. "Hugh forced us to be very organized. He was no nonsense but, at the same time, unobtrusive. He didn't try to make us into his image of us."

Word on the street, and from the lips of people who get paid to keep things positive, was that *In Violet Light* was a collection of great songs and that producer

Padgham had done a masterful job of melding style and substance. Reading between the superlatives, those who got an early listen, were more prone to saying the album was a challenging turn and one that would grow in power with repeated listenings.

In other words, *In Violet Light* was anybody's guess.

While expanding their popularity outside of Canada and, most importantly, into the United States and Europe, continued to be important, the band seemed quite content to let secondary markets slide to a large extent. But that did not mean they had given up trying when, sometime before the release of *In Violet Light*, they signed a distribution deal with well-known independent label Rounder Records to distribute The Hip's music outside of Canada.

The Hip would further cement its long held reputation as Canada's favorite son when, in May 2002, they would be inducted into and placed into the country's Canadian Walk of Fame. "I think we felt pretty awkward about the whole thing," Baker reflected to *Hiponline.com.* "It is an honor to be included in that group of people. It's different when you get up and play your songs and people applaud because they like your songs and that's great! But when you're standing up there [receiving the honor] and people are applauding and you do not have your guitar that is really awkward."

In Violet Light was released June 11, 2002 and the response, as was expected, was mixed.

Many reviews, while positive in tone, were far from glowing. And true to some prognosticators, the album's mixture of rock and pop was far from seamless. The word 'underrated' seemed to be mentioned quite a bit in write-ups. As expected, Hip fans flocked to the record, eventually catapulting it to No. 2 on the Canadian Album chart. The album would also make a brief entry into the US Album chart at a tepid No. 169. Singles would be a whole different story as radio continued its trend of suddenly shunning the band as four singles, "It's a Good Life If You Don't Weaken," "Silver Jet" and "The Darkest One" failed to chart on Canada's Singles chart.

If the lack of radio acceptance was of any concern, the band was not showing it. Because by February, they were already into a monster of a tour that would take in most of the rest of the year and include countless stops in both Canada and the United States.

One thing was certain from the outset, their time apart prior to *In Violet Light* had not interfered with their live performances. If anything, there appeared to be an added punch to their concerts in which the band, subconsciously or not, felt they had something to prove in a performance setting and responded with a larger than life persona that reinforced the fact that The Hip not only could rock with the best of them but had also shown growth in a suddenly expanded lyrical and tone level. The Hip were now part and parcel of a growth spirt over the past two years that showcased their ability to grow and mature while continuing to enhance the very elements of the band that had gotten them there in the first place.

And The Tragically Hip were, in a creative sense, constantly working it. The tour set list contained a healthy slice of *In Violet Light* as well as the expected crowd pleasers from albums gone by. The surprise continued to be the band's uncanny ability to workshop new material nightly and in front of thousands of fans. Fragments of new songs were constantly on display and new ideas were springing spontaneously to the fore, with an eye constantly being cast to the immediate future and the next album.

"The road is absolutely essential for us," reflected Baker in *Hiponline.com* "When you are out there performing the songs live, you are getting new ideas for the new songs. The cycle is just feeding into itself that way."

On a pure emotional level, the highlight of the 2002 tour was easily the band's selection to play a command performance in October for Queen Elizabeth II during her tour of Canada. The Hip, some admitted nerves aside, proved more than capable of playing in front of royalty and the Queen seemed, according to observers, to enjoy the band's renditions of " It's a Good Life, if You Don't Weaken" and "Poets." When asked how it felt to play before the Queen Of England, the band, collectively and quite humble, acknowledged that it had been an honor and it had been a lot of fun.

As had just about everything else had been as The Tragically Hip ended the year on an up note and returned home. Or at least that was the at large impression.

The reality was that The Tragically Hip, in the wake of the *In Violet Light* tour, were suffering no small amount of burnout. As it would turn out, their struggles were centering on the business side of things. When to tour? When to record? The upshot was that the band made the decision to part ways with their longtime manager Jack Gold.

"We did a lot of soul searching during the *In Violet Light* tour and realized that what we really love is the opportunity to perform together and to play together," Sinclair told *The Toledo Blade*. "It was very vindicating for us. We didn't want to lose what the five of us share. When you've been doing this for a long time it becomes like a marriage."

Chapter Sixteen
Alone Again

But it would not be long before the itch returned. Especially when it came to what, creatively and emotionally, had transpired with *Coke Machine Glow*.

Outside of a group of Hip/Downie hardcores who were expected to support anything the enigmatic singer did, *Coke Machine Glow* had received some particularly harsh trashings. He had been called a narcissist. The record, in many corners, had been deemed garbage. But when it came to exploring what he did, the endless possibilities of the written word and his place in that universe, Downie had not been deterred.

"I enjoy the process of writing to a fault," he offered in *GordDownie.com*. "I love solving the puzzle. I'm interested in doing anything that teaches me something. I've found myself writing more than ever."

The consensus was that Downie's increased solo activity was leaving the rest of The Tragically Hip twiddling their collective thumbs. But as Baker offered during a conversation with *Guitar.com*, that was far from the truth. "Everybody has had different things they do. We've all been working with various people. Paul has been working with Hugh Dillion from The Headstones. I've been doing some songwriting with Craig Northie from The Odds. Johnny has been working with a lot of young bands and has produced a couple of records. Everyone has had their little side things going on. But our main focus is on The Hip."

At home after the last tour and dealing with day to day family life had been a time of introspection in which Downie had begun to think of himself as more a creative entity rather than merely a musician and songwriter. But the reality was that the idea that a second solo album might be in the offing had started much sooner than that. Much of the abbreviated tour Downie had done in conjunction with the release of *Coke Machine Glow* had contained a number of songs, some mere fragments and others more polished, that Downie was already picturing for inclusion in a follow up solo effort.

So much so that, in May 2001, Downie and his fellow musical travelers from *Coke Machine Glow* made a five-day pit stop at the Gas Station Studios and laid down much of what would be *Battle of the Nudes*. Downie would mentally live with the songs, in between Hip duties, for the better part of a year before he entered The Bathouse Studios in May 2002 and finally emerged with the 12 songs that would comprise *Battle of the Nudes*.

If anything, *Battle of the Nudes* would turn out to be a looser, freer flowing exercise than Downie's previous solo disc. It was an album that was quite natural and light years away from calculating, with elements of folk and rock weaving in and out of Downie's free thinking and wide ranging lyrics.

Family in all its diverse manifestations was made immediately evident in the song "Into the Night" which tells the quietly fearful tale of a dad's watching as his child goes off into the great unknown. Yet another ode to the complexity of family, "We're Hardcore," tells a tale of obligation and it's just rewards in a very punk, very pent up release of emotion that showcases Downie on the edge. "Pascal's Submarine" is a deft pop exercise in which Downie uses deep French thinker Blaise Pascal's works as a jumping off point for a different take on the Kursk submarine disaster. "Figment" is solid garage rock while "11th Fret" channels the density and tone of David Bowie circa his Berlin period.

"The solo records have been made during periods where I have been closely connected to my daily life," Downie explained to "No Depression." "The records probably reflect the sound of my daily life. I just found the daily life informing the craft and vice-versa."

Battle of the Nudes was a much better produced album than *Coke Machine Glow* and that seemed to weigh heavily in the critical response from the music community. There was a growing sense of appreciation in what Downie was trying to do and where he was going as a solo artist. The album would not come close to matching a typical Hip album in terms of sales and commercial success. But Downie was steadfast in his defense of what *Battle of the Nudes* represented, so much so that he pulled together a 35-day tour to showcase the album as well as a smattering *of Coke Machine Glow* material. The tour, largely in small out of the way and very non Hip level venues in both the US and Canada, was met with good cheer and support from those who had a front row seat on the emergence of Downie in a different place.

The vibe on the *Battle of the Nudes* tour was definitely different. Once the audience got past the idea that this was Gord Downie just doing his own thing rather than all the grandeur and pressure of it being Gord Downie and The Tragically Hip, Downie assumed another identity, that of a simple songsmith, plying his craft. Those privy to these shows saw Downie enraptured and, yet, relaxed in this new cloak.

Downie would look back on his solo efforts with a sense of fulfillment in conversation with "No Depression." "It has been a good run the last bunch of years. It's sort of what I had hoped. I want to be a better musician, a better writer, a stronger writer. I want to be able to catch more stuff as it's going by."

Downie's drive to do more and more became evident shortly after the final song was in the can for *Battles of the Nudes*. By the next morning, he was already writing songs for the next The Tragically Hip album.

If he was creatively drained, he was not showing it.

Chapter Seventeen
Hip Get Rough

In fact, Downie succumbed to a new and different influence during his *Battle of the Nudes* down time between shows. His vision of the world and his surroundings became more global in nature. Through the magic of Fox News, he learned about how Americans, specifically the reigning US president Bush stumbled in and out of world situations with hardly a clue, the bloody consequences of The Iraq War and an increasingly, to Downie, rise of nationalism without rhyme or reason.

Downie was becoming a real world traveler, far removed from the isolation of literature, Canadian thoughts and history and a soft, thoughtful approach to his surroundings. And what he was discovering was often raw and bloody. Downie spent every free moment during the *Battle of the Nudes* tour writing songs that reflected his newfound reality and concern with the madness of it all.

And he would emerge with the core of what would be the album *In Between Evolution*.

Sinclair had a front row seat for Downie's evolution and awareness into a war torn new world and explained to *The Queen's Journal* that he was sympathetic to his singer's plight. "It's hard not to be moved by what they [America] face every day in their media and what they're being told by their leaders. We take that stuff very seriously and Gord was really affected by it. It was a very heavy and serious time when [Downie] was lyrically putting this record together, both within the band but also certainly in the world around us."

To those privy to the inner workings of the band, it was a time of looking back and looking forward, recapturing the spirit of the rocking Hip that produced *Road Apples* and the ambitious moments of *Music @ Work* and *In Violet Light*. It was also a time to reunite as the emotional core of a band. I know, The Tragically Hip always seemed the ideal of a band as family and, without being specific, this family has had its moments of quiet frustration. Sinclair, in conversation with *Canadian Musician*, stated it best when he said "we had moved the ego from the equation enough that none of us felt too precious about what we were doing."

Much of the innate tension within the band had stemmed from compromise on their previous two albums that had left a bad taste in their mouth. Baker dissected that growing frustration in conversation with *Guitar.com*.

"We did a very Pro Tools oriented record, two albums back, where we got into all kinds of crazy shit where you have 120 tracks on one song and we delayed all of our mixing decisions. So we wanted to avoid that. And then on the last record we had a great producer but he was very frank about the idea of 'I hate guitar solos. No guitar solos.' And that's kind of what we do. So as much as we enjoyed the experience, we decided that this time we had to work with a real guitar guy, a guitar, bass and drums kind of producer."

Which was when Adam Kasper entered the picture. Kasper, out of Seattle, had a long and distinguished career defending the rights of rockers to realistically apply their craft. His producer and engineering credits include Aerosmith, Nirvana, Foo Fighters, Queens of the Stone Age, REM and Pearl Jam.

In turn, Kasper did his homework, listening to enough of The Hip's recorded output to get a sense of where the band had been and enough fragments of Downie's new lyrics to have a sense of where the group was now heading. Essentially the issue the band would be running on was a quasi-militant stance against war and all forms of conflict done up in deep and, as conceived in the band's earliest preparation, yet punchy rock and roll journey into such concepts as commitment and death. Kasper had a real sense of where The Tragically Hip were going with *In Between Evolution* and, as Baker remembered in his *Guitar.com* interview, seeing the band live sealed the deal.

"Adam came and saw the band and he said 'You guys have great chemistry and the trick is to try and capture that in the studio.' Of course you can't capture a live gig in the studio. But you try and keep the chemistry intact and he was definitely after the same things that we were after. We felt confident enough to give him free reign to mess with anything or if he had any suggestions."

Kasper's first suggestion was that The Hip move from comfortable and exotic recording locals to the producer's very rock and roll studio in Seattle, the scene of many of Kasper's recording successes and conducive to the very live sound the band envisioned for *In Between Evolution*. The band also decided that playing a couple of live gigs just before entering the studio would engrain the sense of 'live' in the band as well as test drive the new songs in front of a flesh and blood audience.

Langlois emphasized the importance of this performing wrinkle in conversation with *The Toledo Blade*. "Playing live is what comes naturally to us. By playing a couple of gigs in front of people before going into the studio, we were able to give both the audience and us exactly what we needed."

There was a definite homage to the album *Road Apples* in the recording sessions for *In Between Evolution*. This time around, The Tragically Hip were reduced to their most primal, five guys standing around, playing live in a large recording studio. No overdubs or nods to the latest technology, the album was put together in a very traditional sounding rock and roll sense. Baker explained it more succinctly and colorful in an interview with *The Rochester City Newspaper* when he offered, "You have your songs, you tour the shit out of them so they're road ready and so by the time you get them in the studio, and it's just a matter of setting up and playing them."

While 'touring the shit out of them' may have been a colorful over-exaggeration, The Hip would prove diligent in prepping their new material as well as ramping up for what would be another lengthy 2004 tour. Beginning in February 2003 and concluding in October 2003, the band would spread out a total of six warm up shows in various Canadian locals. Consequently, by the time *In Between Evolution* was being recorded, the seeds of familiarity had been effectively planted in audience's psyches and the band had a firm grip on performing them for what would be a very long haul.

In hindsight, *In Between Evolution* seemed to exorcise a number of demons. The Hip relished the notion of literally recording live and the idea that most of the songs had been reduced to their primitive rock and roll state. The sessions would be the ideal petri dish for songs that were straying wildly from preconceived notions. The longest song on the album clocked in at a brisk 4:34, just enough time to proclaim new attitudes and commitments. "Heaven is a Better Place Today" proved a subtle yet telling two pronged assault, chronicling both the 2003 invasion of Iraq and the emergence of born again patriotism. "One Night in Copenhagen," which featured the lyrics "you talentless fuck/good fucking luck" that earned the album the band's first parental advisory sticker, was a solid diatribe against the consequences of celebrity. "Gus: The Polar Bear from Central Park," an in-your-face shot at confinement, is both melancholy and message heavy, a truly rare feat that the band pulls off in grand manner. The Tragically Hip emerged from Kasper's studio with an album that had monster hit written all over it.

In Between Evolution was released on June 29, 2004. The album immediately shot to No. 1 on Canada's album chart, selling a reported 22,500 copies during its first week out. Things looked promising. But the lack of a single on the radio (three singles would be released but none would end up in Canadian radio rotation and would fail to chart), inevitable mixed reviews and, in many critical quarters, the dark nature of many of the songs, would drag sales down by 50 percent during the album's second week. Of small consolation was that *In Between Evolution*, thanks in no small part to US distributor Rounder Records, made a brief appearance on the US Heat chart at No. 18. The album would be praised as the best pure rock album by the band since *Road Apples* and would ultimately join its predecessor in being certified platinum by September 2004.

The band celebrated going platinum on the road. No surprise there. As a matter of fact, The Hip had been so anxious to showcase their new music on a grand scale by beginning what would be a seven-month jaunt through the US and Canada that they set off a full week before the release of *In Between Evolution*. From the moment they hit the road, there were encouraging signs that the band, however you wanted to slice it, now fit the definition of superstars, albeit in their own subtle way.

A tone of fun loving and unexpected would permeate the tour, as witness a special fan club member only invite to The Mod Club that saw the band in a loose much smaller environment that brought out the free and easy nature of a Hip performance and set the tone for the tour proper which would start a few days later.

Canada remained a given. North of the border they could do no wrong. But the logistics now required to transport the band and their show, and the ever-increasing size of the venues, were now the barometer by which only upper echelon acts were measured. The

US portion of the tour, however, was where the rubber, creatively, was hitting the road. Record sales were still only a fraction of what Canada typically turned but *In Between Evolution* was appearing to be the album that had kicked open American markets another notch. South of the border it was still primarily clubs and small halls but, bottom line, even the most fringe US fans seemed to know the words to "Vaccine Scar" and "It Can't Be Nashville Every Night."

The tour was conspicuous by its really 'cool' moments for the band. The band celebrated Canada Day on July 1 with a reported manic performance that would be duplicated ten days later as an attractive element of the Wasaga Beach Blues Festival. The band's long held support for Canadian sports found an opportunity on November 21 when The Hip entertained a stadium full of fanatics with a rousing halftime show on the occasion of the 92nd Grey Cup game.

But easily one of the more memorable moments of the *In Between Evolution* tour would be time off the road when The Hip indulged themselves in a bit of a lark, playing themselves in a cameo in the popular Canada TV series *Corner Gas*. In their scene, the band, playing a nondescript garage band are rehearsing in a cramped studio when the show regulars show up and kick the band out of the studio.

Adding insult to injury, they steal their amps.

Chapter Eighteen
Who Are Hip?

The Tragically Hip were never one of those bands that deliberately courted controversy. But in October 2005, controversy definitely had the band in their sights.

The song *"New Orleans is Sinking"* had become a standard of sorts on numerous Canadian radio stations and could be found in regular rotation at just about any time of the day or night. But the song became reality when Hurricane Katrina struck the city of New Orleans in September and seemingly hitting way too close to the band's lyrical assessment of a city under siege. A number of radio stations immediately succumbed to a bad case of sensitivity and social correctness and immediately pulled the song from their playlist.

One of those who yanked the song off the air was Gord Taylor, program director of radio station 106.9 The Bear who told *Jam,* "We'll sit on the song for a while until the situation cools off. We planned to play the song days before Katrina struck. It just happened to land on our schedule before we realized the full impact of the storm. It wasn't a conscious decision to play *"New Orleans is Sinking"* just as the city was really sinking."

All good intentions aside, a number of Tragically Hip fans took offense at the notion of anything keeping them from one of their favorite songs and, as a result, a number of pirate radio stations scattered throughout Canada, began playing "New Orleans is Sinking" in direct defiance of corporate radio stations. As it would turn out, the members of the band were alternately bemused and frustrated at what they considered a misrepresentation of what the lyrics were saying. Not surprisingly, Downie was thrust into the center of the controversy and, in a 2005 radio interview, patiently explained, "The core message of the song is positive. It praises the spirit of the city that cannot be beaten and will certainly rise again." Fay told *Live Daily.com* that "We had people in Canada and they said they were not going to play that song. But if you did the history of the city, like the band and particularly Gord did, you would know that New Orleans was always expecting the big one."

Eventually the radio stations bowed to pressure and reinstated "New Orleans is Sinking" to their playlists. This dust up would turn out to be the high point of what had been shaping up as a fairly laidback year for the band. The band conceded that family time and the need to mentally and creatively regroup was important at that point. They were always working on songs but, for the moment, a direction was not quickly forthcoming and there seemed to be no hurry. A mini-tour of Canada, seven shows scattered out between January and December of 2005, would be the extent of their road endeavors.

That the Tragically Hip had arrived at a state of grace as Canada's national treasure and a career whose longevity had been marked by consistent turns in progressing the rock and roll arts would find validation in 2005 with their selection to the Canadian Rock and Roll Hall of Fame. Fay recalled the moment when becoming anointed rock royalty was officially theirs. "It was kind of weird but it was also kind of cool. We walked down the red carpet and there were all these young bands. But we knew we still had gas in the tank. It was a little crazy until we released that both Rush and Neil Young were already in the hall. Then it was just cool."

Not surprisingly humble at the honor, the band's attitude remained what could they do next and what could they do better. In the case of Baker, the time off from all things Hip afforded the guitarist to take the long fomenting step into his own world with· a solo project that would go under the banner of *Stripper's Union*.

Late in 2004, Baker was feeling restless enough to ring up one of his many musical friends Craig Northey, formerly of the band The Odds. They got together, talked a lot of shop and spent hours going through stacks of songs Baker had written but never found their way onto Hip records, largely due to Downie's lyrical domination. "I'm a guitar player," Baker said in an interview with *Artist Trove.com*. "I love collaboration. So I called up some friends and said let's do something."

With the addition of Odds' alum Doug Elliott and Pat Steward, *Stripper's Union* was born, a straightforward rock and roll animal of the old school, equal parts Iggy Pop and Tom Petty that would conform to Baker's long held musical beliefs. "Sincere music is about the approach," Baker offered to *Artist Trove.com*. "It has nothing to do with the flash. It's about everybody playing a small role in trying to create a big, pulsating thing."

With 13 songs in hand, *Stripper's Union* repaired to The Bathouse Studio and emerged a scant ten days later with the straight ahead rock and roll that would become the album entitled *Stripper's Union Local 518*. The album would come and go with little recognition, other than the notoriety of a Hip member going solo. But Baker was thrilled with the fact that he could go into the studio with new musicians and play out in a respectable manner. "Everyone was feeling each other out, figuring out exactly what this [the album] was going to be. We were successful in pushing in different directions to see what would work."

While fairly idle during 2005, The Hip were not above pushing some band product as it came to the end of the year. Traditionally, the Christmas selling season was filled to overflowing with greatest hits packages and bands doing Christmas covers. But The Tragically Hip were not about to take the predictable way out. And so, the first week in November saw a literal rush of extremely fan friendly releases.

First out of the chute was a monster of a limited edition collection called *Hipeonymous,* witch, as contained in a hardcover book shell, contained more Hip than even the diehard fan could shake a stick at. To wit: A two CD compilation of remastered fans' favorite Hip tunes (as voted on by the fans) entitled *Yer Favourites*, which also included two brand new songs "No Threat" and "The New Maybe." A full-length concert DVD called *That Night in Toronto*, a backstage documentary, a DVD of all the band's music videos and, finally, an original short film called *The Right Whale* that featured an original score written by the band. Meant more as a gift to the fans than anything else, nobody was more surprised than the band when *Hipeonymous* charted on the Canada charts at No.4 and would eventually go platinum.

With their label always looking at the bottom line, *Yer Favourites* would be released as a separate entity a week after *Hipeonymous*.as a more commercially viable package. In that context *Yer Favourites* did the job, making it to No. 1 on the Canadian *Billboard* charts and also going platinum. The label made a fairly weak attempt at breaking the song "No Threat" as a chart single but the stations were having none of it and the single failed to chart.

The Tragically Hip have never been what you would call a high drama kind of band. In fact, they've only ever slightly blown a gasket when it's come to creative issues and then it was the equivalent of a pin drop. Such was the case going into 2006. Despite the fact that *In Between Evolution* was considered a mild success, the album was still considered a plateau that they band could, to that point, not get beyond. What they had happily taken away from that album was their newfound affinity for recording primarily live and returning to their rock roots that, to this day, makes *Road Apples* one of The Hip's most treasured albums. Indirectly, it would be *Yer Favourites* that would steer the band in their latest direction. Those prone to research were quick to point out that a good percentage of the fans selections were rock numbers drawn from the band's earlier albums. The Hip could take a hint

So it was those attitudes that were guiding the band as they laid the groundwork for *World Container*. There was the temptation to return to Kasper for *World Container* but the fates would eventually step in and offer up Bob Rock. Rock, likewise Canadian born and bred, was well known as the go-to producer for rock, metal and punk, having produced albums for the likes of The Cult, Motley Crüe, Bon Jovi and Metallica. Of the latter group, Rock had turned the knobs on half a dozen albums and had recently come to an amicable, but ultimately stressful parting of the ways.

Needless to say, bands have always lined up around the block to get Rock to turn the knobs. And Rock jokingly acknowledged in a conversation with the *Toronto Sun* that, these days, the criterion for taking a job is simple. "I think it really comes down to who I want to spend four months with."

Long story short, The Tragically Hip were not on the producer's radar in 2006. But his manager Bruce Allen, who made no bones about the fact that he never thought much of the band, had cultivated a change of heart and pushed his newfound enthusiasm onto Rock. "Allen was the guy who pushed The Tragically Hip," Rock told *The Toronto Sun*. "He told me that these guys are a great band and that there was a reason why they were still around. He told me that they just needed to make a better record and that I was the one he thought could do it."

For their part, the band was familiar with Rock's credit but were a bit hesitant when Allen arranged a phone call between Rock and Downie. The pair agreed to talk.

"Bob was in his home in Maui and I was in an

Indian restaurant in Toronto," Downie related in a *Hipfans.com* interview. "We talked very easily about music, kids and just different things. At the end of it we agreed that I would fly out to Maui [where Rock lived.]"

Downie hopped a plane and arrived on Maui with a handful of Tragically Hip CD's in hand. They drove around Maui, Rock listened to the CD's and they bounced ideas back and forth about what the producer might bring to the table. Both realized by the end of the singer's visit that the pair had real chemistry. Downie was encouraged enough that he invited Rock back to Vancouver for further discussion and to meet with the rest of the band.

"So I talked to Gord," Rock told *The Toronto Sun*, "and then I went to Vancouver and I met the guys. It was like a dream come true."

Downie seconded that emotion when he gushed to *Hipfans.com* "We were awed by his instincts and abilities. I'd never met anyone like him. He was a rock and roller, a true music lover through and through."

This meeting of the minds led to what seemed an ambitious, if somewhat nebulous goal. To make an album that was truly Canadian in tone and to have fun at the same time. And in a recording odyssey that ultimately led The Hip through studios in Maui, Toronto and Vancouver, band and producer seemed to be accomplishing that goal. The promise of positive give and take between Rock and the band was immediately realized. There was a lot of variations on "why don't we try this" and "how about if we do it this way?" In the best possible way, the vibe during the recording of *World Container* was both reckless and courageous. So much so that nobody balked when such odd choices as the glockenspiel, synthesizer and harpsichord were sprinkled throughout the band's straight ahead rock and roll sound.

Fay described the studio experience and working with Rock as "awesome." "He gets involved with everything. He sort of hones in on the parts. It was very much an organic experience. He didn't want us to know the songs too much. He wanted sort of rough ideas so none of our bad habits would set in. We wouldn't spend much more than six or seven takes getting a track."

Lyrically, everything hinged on Downie's mood at the moment and, the surprise was that, for the first time in a long time, he was addressing an emotion on the songs "Pretend" and "Last Night I Dreamed You Didn't Love Me" that had eluded him for ages and that he was suddenly determined to rediscover.

"I decided I'd avoided the elephant in the room, love, long enough," he explained to *Canoe.com*. "I'd just ignored it because love's been done to death. When you start poking around it though, it's the taking the crack at it that's the thing. I had to find out what it, love, meant to me."

Throughout the sessions, it appeared that many of the songs were appearing as trademark Hip, albeit with a new coat of paint. Easily the biggest turnabout was the song "The View," something so bright, sunny, poppy and radio friendly that it appeared almost a shock to long time Hip fans' sensibilities. That it worked as well as it did owed much to the decision to bring in keyboard player Jamie Edwards for the song's tantalizing hook. What would turn out to be the wildly popular ode to hockey and real life, "The Lonely End of the Rink," was made all the more dazzling by elements of disco, reggae and more than enough U2 asides to spice up the proceedings. "The Drop Off "provided a nice piece of vocal largesse as Downie snapped out of his quasi manic emoting long enough to try his hand at rapping the song's chorus. But it would not be The Hip without at least one full on blow against the empire and with the album's title track, "World Container," Downie's long growing love affair with saving the planet was in full flower as he delivered a passionate yet smart assault on the lax environmental attitude and, in particular, Canada's conservative government.

By the time, the band emerged from the *World Container* sessions, it was a given that The Hip had come up with an album that played upon both the band's traditional rock values as well and some new thoughts and actions. Nobody was saying that *World Container* could be the album to break the slide of sales and increase their viability outside of Canada and their slow but sure growth in the United States.

At least nobody was saying it publically.

The band and the label knew it was important to get *World Container* off to a flying start and took great pains to get the word out well before its October 17 release. The first single "The View" was released well ahead of the album and immediately shot to No. 1 on the Canadian Singles chart, ending the string of non-charting Hip singles. In another bit of cross promotion, the song "The Lonely End of the Rink" was premiered October 7 on the show *Hockey Night in Canada*. That early exposure worked as World Container debuted at

No. 2 on the Canadian Album chart (when released in the States some months later, the album would climb to No. 11 on the US Heat chart). The single "World Container" would do amazingly well by Canada standards, selling 27,000 copies in its first week of release and being certified platinum by the end of October. That three other singles, "The Lonely End of The Rink," "Yer Not the Ocean" and "Family Band" would subsequently fail to chart was a minor blemish amid the rush of largely positive reviews and sales. In the often cynical dollars and cents world of music, *World Container* had put The Tragically Hip back on track.

And back on the road. Beginning in May and on through to the end of the year, The Hip crossed Canada and, sporadically, into the United States, with a quick jump across the pond for a pair of shows in Holland. Touring at this point was a fairly predictable routine but one the band continued to embrace. The venues were now much bigger, the audiences were enthusiastic in their continued support of the band and the shows continued to surprise with old favorites mixed in with obscure deep cuts and improvisational workouts on new songs being worked out. But this tour would have the extra kick when, along the way, the band hooked up as opening act for yet another legendary rock band.

The Who.

The particulars of this gig which would ultimately grow to include several US dates, a tour of eastern Canada and some shows in Europe was a lot of good fun and excitement for The Hip. Opening for one of their idols that they grew up listening to, relieved of

158

the inherent pressure of being the headlining act and watching one of the greatest bands in rock history work it out night after night was literally the ultimate rock and roll dream.

Fay was enthusiastic when he recalled that opportunity of a lifetime in conversation with *Live Daily.com* "We played with Page and Plant. We played with The Stones. When the opportunity came to play with The Who, we didn't have to think twice…

"…We just jumped on it."

Chapter Nineteen
Hip Are Who They Are

And going into 2007 The Tragically Hip continued to jump. Rather than unwind for a time after a long tour that had included an extended period opening for The Who, the band definitely had road fever. Especially Hip drummer Fay who extolled the virtues of living out of a suitcase with *The Queens Journal*.

"I think touring can really burn a person out but, for others, it's really where their lives make sense. I like the process of being on the road, moving to the next place and thinking about the next town you're going to. It's cool. It's therapeutic."

Beginning in January and ending in November, The Tragically Hip crisscrossed Canada, the United States and added a short jaunt in Europe to the tune of 103 shows. Almost as an afterthought, they ended their marathon touring schedule in 2008 with a comparatively short tour of seven shows between February and July with occasional shows near year's end.

The shows were reportedly vintage Hip, on any given performance the band played a lot of *World Contai*ner and *In Between Evolution* and a generous helping of their greatest hits as well as the occasional obscurity. And, as if to test their mettle as a touring band, The Hip reportedly rocked the house pretty much every night. There was much speculation as to why the band, now in their prime, would push so hard. *World Container* had been a comeback album for The Hip after a down period, commercially, and they band, in a live setting could not be blamed for wanting to ride that pony for all it was worth. There was the fact that the band acknowledged to being their best, creatively and emotionally, when they were playing live. And those who saw the band regularly during that 2007-2008 marathon most certainly knew that there was a lot of on the job woodshedding going on.

Which was good because The Tragically Hip's stint as road warriors had put the band behind schedule for their next album. The Hip had always been workmanlike when it came to getting new music out. A new album every two years had been their mantra. And by the time they entered 2008, they were officially behind schedule.

Part of the delay may well have centered on Downie. Always writing and reconfiguring his lyrical worldview, The Hip singer, at this time, seemed intent on a new and emotional psychological path, one alternately far-reaching and reclusive. Age may well have had something to do with it as the band members, collectively, were by now well into their middle to late 40's and middle age can do some strange things to people's heads. And when you're a man of words, as Downie explained to *The Buffalo News*, thoughts can get kind of all over the place.

"I'm still sort of exploring what it all means,"

said the cryptic singer. "I'm still kind of finding out what it can mean, something on a few levels. I like the idea of hopeful and defiant. It's something you might say to calm down a rioting crowd. It's the things we're all hoping to hear."

And it was not just Downie. The rest of the band was also beginning to see things a little bit differently. They were still rock and rollers at heart and always would be. But, taking their cues from Downie, the collective sound was taking on new senses of depth and emotion. Suddenly everything did not have to be straightforward and hard charging. Subtlety and free ranging, sometimes acoustic, sometimes folk and a little bit country, was making its presence felt as the songs began to round into shape.

Given these new turns, it would be rather surprising when the band returned to Rock to produce *We Are the Same*. The producer got points for turning the band around on a number of levels, not the least was commercial viability. But Rock was (no pun intended) a rock guy and *We Are the Same* was shaping up as anything but.

"I think after doing *World Container* we were pretty happy with the results and it seemed like we got to know each other just as the album was ending," Rock said on *Tragically Hip.com* and, later, in the *Niagara Falls Review*. "We kind of figured out what everybody did and stuff. We just knew that we had to try to at least raise the bar a little bit."

With the 2008 tour dates becoming more sporadic, The Hip and Rock began meeting at the band's Bathouse Studio. As was usually the case, those early days consisted largely of working on a seemingly endless number of songs and finally whittling them down to the final cut that would make the album. But once the band got down to business, the collective vibe in the studio was that of head scratching because, for both the producer and the band, *We Are the Same* was very much a mystery.

If the album was crying out for more of the same and the expected, it quickly became evident that this was not that album. There were no heavy blues guitar riffs to hang simple songs on. There was a sense of simplicity and light, quiet, softer and, yes, prettier sounds were the order of the day. The songs were slow to the point that The Hip often had to question whether they were truly the band they had played in for decades. That band did not pander with lots of acoustic/folk/country influences. This band did. In the past, things like soft acoustic guitar, lush orchestration and strings were an alien life form. In *We Are the Same*, they were the key that unlocked a new direction.

Whatever that new direction would turn out to be.

They band was making the point that it was determined to try something different, no matter the cost. The song *Morning Moon* was a good-natured hodge-podge of the experimentation abroad in the studio. Part folk, part country, understated soft guitar licks and a whole lot of strings. Rock and roll was barely a blip on the radar on this song. "Honey Please" was a pleasant enough romantic interlude with only the interplay between mandolin and a slide guitar passage to give the song a pulse. It would take "Queen Of the Furrows" to indicate that The Hip had not completely given up their trademark sound for lent. "Frozen in My Tracks" may well have been the truest hybrids that largely worked.

Reasonably handled pop/rock melancholia that, at mid song, evolves into a crazy kind of waltz.

But easily the bravest song on the album would also be the longest song the band ever recorded. At 9:27, "The Depression Suite" was a three-part lyrical/historical mélange, one that paid homage to the great depression and the trials and tribulations of those who toiled in the oil. Industry. The band's instrumentation worked tirelessly and mostly effectively in capturing the abrupt changes in each segment of the odyssey and playing on the human emotions and costs. Lyrically Downie was writing at a staccato pitch, laying out slices of passion and irony, working, largely successfully, as a powerful anchor to the music.

Downie felt in his gut that "The Desperation Suite" would set the tone and attitude in which *We Are the Same* would present itself and recalled as much in conversation with *Maclean's*. "Our producer had the idea to try and combine three songs. It was Paul [Langlois] idea to take three particular songs and the whole process was instantaneous. Then it just became a practical matter of how do we stitch three songs together and make them flow? I gave it the name "The Depression Suite" as a bit of a laugh but it stuck. I think with this record we have pushed the margins a bit wider and "The Depression Suite" helped us do that."

We Are the Same was completed in October 2008.

As with the previous album, The Hip knew that they would need to give *We Are the Same* a bit of a jump start. In February 2009, two months ahead of the release of *We Are the Same,* the band released the first single, "Love is a First," to radio stations. It would prove a fairly safe first strike as "Love is a First" would top out at No. 22 on the Canadian Singles chart. As had become a pattern with previous albums, two more attempts at chart singles, "Morning Moon" and "Speed River" would fail to chart. To further advance word of mouth on the new album, The Hip entered into a onetime deal with Canada's Cineplex Theaters in which they would play a live concert in their Bathouse Recording Studio that would be simulcast to a number of movie theaters throughout Canada.

The album would be released on April 7, 2009 and would follow a pattern similar to that of *World Container*. *Same* would sell 27,000 copies in its first week out and would debut at No. 1 on the Canadian Album chart. Once again, US interest was negligible with the album topping out at No. 148 on the US Album chart. As expected reviews were decidedly mixed with many critics felling a sense of bewilderment and a certain amount of betrayal at how far the band had strayed from its roots while giving measured applause for the experimentation inherent in the album. *We Are the Same* would ultimately be one of the toughest Tragically Hip albums to critically put a finger on. It would take years of discussion and disagreement and, at the end of the day, opinions would remain divided.

The band wasted little time in getting on the road, an ambitious tour of Canada, the United States and an increasing number of dates in Europe. One new wrinkle that the band decided on was that their sets would be much longer as explained by Downie in *Billboard.* "We plan to play lengthy shows with an intermission in the middle. We did that once about ten years ago. I think we decided with this album we needed to do something where we could expand the margins and really work on the dynamics."

The response to the *We Are the Same* songs in a live setting went down quite well on the tour. Despite the predictable lack of sales, US audiences had come to appreciate the band live and, particularly on this tour, the expansive/sonic nature of the new material went down especially well. When it came to the European dates, especially the four shows in London, it was like discovering a brave new world for the band. The songs from *We Are the Same* were right up UK fans' attitudes when it came to the pop/quirky elements of the songs and were met with enthusiastic responses night after night. Ditto The Hip's long time stronghold of Holland and Belgium where the support was there when seemingly nobody else across the pond gave a damn.

Downie drew the parallels to the live vs. recorded version of *We Are the Same* in a conversation with the *Ottawa Citizen*. "The songs live are different from the new album which is good. Live, we have to make the songs wild and wooly and disrespect them a little bit or, at least, just try and lose the need to emulate the record. After all, it's rock and roll."

Chapter Twenty
Hip Breaks

For The Tragically Hip, 2010 through 2011 would be time off for good behavior. At least as it pertained to touring. After the marathon tour behind *We Are the Same*, there would be no shows scheduled through 2010 and a mere 14 dates through 2011. Which is not to say that the band was not busy.

The first time in a long time was seeing the band leading the life of landed gentlemen, spending a lot of time being normal family men, attending to the everyday issues of being a husband and father. But that did not mean that The Hip had put their music aside. Ideas for future Hip albums were constantly flying back and forth. And, perhaps more importantly to their creative spirit, the individual members of the band were immersed in a variety of solo projects.

Downie was apparently the one who needed non-Hip therapy in the worst way as he explained in an interview with *CTV.com*. "We made two Hip albums in fairly quick succession and I remember saying to my wife that I was really going to commit to that and try to do as good a job as possible. There was just no time."

But midway through 2009, Downie suddenly found himself with the time and the feeling that would ultimately translate to his third solo album, *The Grand Bounce*. "My family influences everything in my life," he told *CTV.com*. "They inspire everything I do. Everything I eat. Everything I don't eat. You settle into the fact that you let this kids affect you in great and positive ways and that can only affect your work in great and positive ways."

The good feeling extended to his de facto solo band, Country of Miracles who had helped him through his two previous solo outings. And there was also the good memory of meeting and developing a rapport with Death Cab for Cutie guitarist and well-known producer Chris Walla in 2008. Bringing up those memories two years later helped fuel Downie's desire to proceed with *The Grand Bounce* with Walla at the helm. "It just got some hunches rolling," he recalled to *The Toronto Star*. "I thought he'd really get along with the guys from Country of Miracles and I thought his sonic sense would mesh with their sense of spirit. They all got along famously."

Walla agreed in principle to produce *The Grand Bounce*. Which, in turn, resulted in the pair getting together and going through countless Downie compositions. Walla offered suggestions on where the songs should go and it all made sense to the singer and the band.

The Grand Bounce sessions convened in August 2009 at the by now familiar confines of The Bathouse Studio. It was in the spirit of what Downie described as "camaraderie, friendship and spirit" that 13 songs were knocked out in a period of two weeks.

Although there were occasional, and not totally unexpected, asides to the Hip's lyrical and subtle instrumentation, *The Grand Bounce* sessions were decidedly Downie's in tone. "Yellow Days" was typical of the vibe that had been set adrift, a mystical dance layered over the notion of leisurely time and space. *"Moon Over Glenora"* was a moving yet sensitive excursion into the manifestation of good times. "The Dance and Its Disappearance" hinted a tensions moving just below the surface but filtered through the vibe of a calm lakeside afternoon with family and friends.

Walla did his job. His subtle wash of studio polish made effective points in bolstering the overall production. The attitude of simple was never far from the proceedings but Walla's talents were immediately evident in what turned out to be Downie's smoothest sounding solo album to date.

Downie's faith in the simple things of life would be rewarded with the release of *The Grand Bounce* on June 8, 2010. The album would rise to No. 8 on the Canadian Album chart.

Baker also had the itch to go it alone. And he had the road Jones to prove it. The guitarist loved his family but after nine months on the road, he explained to *Canoe.com* that was having trouble readjusting to domesticity. "I was feeling really creative after all that time on the road and it was hard for me to just slip back into family life. I'd been on tour where, when the sun comes up, it was time to go to bed. And for the first month back home, that was what I was doing."

But when he discovered that both Downie and Langlois were already using their hiatus from Hip to put out solo projects, he knew what he had to do. "At that point, I was looking at sitting around for a year of sitting around doing nothing and getting fat. So I knew that, when I was up, the house would be quiet and everyone was asleep, I could just slip down to the basement and plug away."

Baker eventually got three songs where he wanted them and looked up his cohort from the previous *Stripper's Union* album, Craig Northey. Northey was up for another album. The problem was logistic in nature as Northey was based in Vancouver and Baker in Kingston. The problem was solved when they agreed to meet somewhat half way at a motel in Smith Falls, Ontario, where, over a period of days, they hammered out the lyrics to Baker's initial offerings.

"I felt good about that," Baker recalled to *Canoe.com*. "That's what happens when the two of us get together, stuff tumbles out that feels so easy and natural. I thought 'Okay we've got a start at three. I assembled a bunch more ideas and in April I went to Vancouver and we worked on things in Craig's studio." The result was an earthy mixture of songs and influences that ran the gamut from Stax Vault style rhythm and blues, to country, pop and guitar heavy rock and roll.

Baker's second *Stripper's Union* album, *The Deuce*, was released in June 2011 to solid reviews for Baker and his side project. Stripper's Union also managed a series of live shows in support of the album that showed that Baker could definitely rock in a non-Hip way.

For Langlois, the road to doing other than Hip

work was a long and comfortable one. After nearly three decades playing behind his fellow bandmates, the self-effacing guitarist seemed quite happy out of the spotlight. "I'm comfortable with that," he confessed to *The Toronto Sun*. "I'm in a role. I'm part of a team. So I think it probably makes it a little bit more difficult for me to step out."

But 'step out' he would finally do in early 2010 and it would be almost by accident rather than design. Ever the team player, Langlois had been working on some ideas for the next Tragically Hip album and had decided to book some time in the band's Bathouse Studio to experiment with some demos on some of the better ones. Away from The Hip and the inherent expectations, Langlois' ideas began to take on a different, encouraging perspective. Before he knew it, the guitarist began thinking he might just have a solo album on his hands.

"I brought my drum kit into the studio," he told *The Toronto Star*. "It took me a day and a half to even get up the courage to sit behind the kit because I really didn't know whether it was going to go well or not. Once the drumming went well I said 'okay I can try singing this.' As it turned out, I was not as uncomfortable with the sound of my own voice as I thought I was going to be. At the end of it, I realized that I had a finished song here."

Before he realized it, what would become the album *Fix This Head* had evolved into a one-man operation with Langlois playing all the instruments and singing? The album, which would be released online December 7, 2010 was followed a physical album early in 2011. On such songs as "Broken Road" and "Can't Wait Anymore," Langlois presented a moody, often dark pop sound that was driven by his long developed country influences. However, Langlois reflected that there were no deep, dark secrets to his going solo.

"In the end I just went with songs I could believe in."

Sinclair, contrary to the solo albums of his bandmates, was quite content to work behind the scenes and below the radar. As a producer and performer he added both music and production to the 2010 Jim Bryson and the Weakerthans album *The Falcon Lake Incident* and, in 2011, he helped with the writing and arranging of The Trews album *Hope and Ruin*.

Ultimately the Hip's solo excursions would have a positive effect on the individual members. Creative muscles suitably flexed. By end of 2011, they were all anxious to get back to their day job.

"We're definitely better for it," said Baker to *Canoe.com*. "Everyone comes back to The Hip after doing their thing totally invigorated. One of the things about these little, side projects is that I'm sure people will say it's a vanity project or they're moonlighting or whatever. For me, it's an absolutely creative outlet."

Chapter Twenty-One
That Sinking Feeling

Downie has never been one to make his personal life public. In fact, the band as a whole have been notorious for keeping non-Hip issues out of the public eye. Which is why it came as a shock that Downie, in 2012, revealed in an interview with George Stroumboulopoulos that all the while he had been working on *The Grand Bounce* and prepping for the band's next album, *Now for Plan A*, he had been in personal hell.

His wife Laura had been diagnosed with breast cancer.

"There were a lot of emotions," said Downie. "You know...anger, fear, impatience. Impatience was a big one. Love...You're just clamoring to help. It was hard to write during all that because that felt, somehow, not right."

Going through her own emotions following the diagnosis and resultant treatment, Laura still was able to muster the creative support she had always had for her husband. She begged Downie not to use the occasion of her disease to "make a cancer album." Which only added to the mental anguish of the singer who was trying to balance being loving and creative. "Writing became a real dilemma," he confessed to *The*

Globe & Mail. "I didn't want to do it. I didn't see the point in doing it. It was me trying to help, mutely, in that way a man around breast cancer tries to help. I questioned whether my work on the album was reflecting my love and devotion to my wife. Nothing was cutting it in that regard. Anything I had done to that point did not seem applicable. It was a struggle."

Downie's faith was rewarded when, almost a year to the day Laura was diagnosed, and she responded to treatment and had gone into remission. *Now for Plan A* could now proceed but the year of emotional turmoil surrounding his wife's illness had colored his approach to songwriting.

Downie seemed to be playing mental games with himself as well as any expectations the band's fans might have. He admits that a lot of the melodies and lyrics for the album were written rather quickly. That rush seemed to have, indirectly, forged a tight and, more often than not, enticing juxtaposition with the band's harsher rock tendencies.

Baker found the idea of what *Now for Plan A* was going to be about a lot easier to pin down in a conversation with *The Post Standard.* "I think there are themes of friendship and themes of getting on with stuff. You know, putting aside petty differences and getting on with stuff."

In many quarters it was a given that, after two records that had seemingly put the band back on the commercial road, Rock would once again come aboard to produce. But as had always seemed the case, The Hip was always looking for creative greener pastures and, instead, went with another Canadian Gavin Brown. Brown had an equally star-studded career in the arena of pop and more radio friendly songs which gave those hoping for another Hip hard charger. But the band was convinced that Brown could handle *Now for Plan A*.

The album was conceived as a quick hit, ten days of recording at The Bathouse Studios, 11 songs. The consensus was that the album was shaping up as a hodge-podge collection of songs with no rhyme or reason to them. But Downie, in *Popmatters.com*, saw things a bit differently. "It's a political album that is committed to the common good. It's a life in a day, politically and personally, through the lens of a relationship."

Deep thoughts but as the songs played out, it seemed that a lot of happenstance and improvisation were a foot. Songs like "About This Map," "At Transformation" and "Man, Machine Poem" seemed a constant mélange of minimalist and over wrought lyrics, odd and irregular melodic twists and turns and loud, occasionally bordering on arena rock, instrumentation and sudden muscular turns all seemingly joined at the Hip (again no pun intended).

It seemed inevitable that Downie's wife's illness would come into play at some point and it did with the song "The Lookahead" looked at the notion of sickness and recovery in a hopeful, yet philosophical way. Downie simply defined it, as "You know everything's going to be alright No matter what."

The first sign that *Now for Plan A* was going to be a tough sell came with the news that the total running time of the album, 39:18 was the shortest Tragically Hip album to date. That coupled with the early buzz that the album could be a bit contrary and inconsistent was already making the prospects of a success a bit dicey. A May 18 release of "At Transformation" as the first single debuted at a disappointing No. 63 on the Canadian Singles chart while a second single "Streets Ahead" was released in August to zero interest and a washout on the charts.

After much anticipation, primarily from the band's label, *Now for Plan A* was released on October 2, 2012. The early reviews were all over the place and covered the critical bases, good, bad and indifferent, pretty thoroughly. The album was also met with a bit of 'so' when it sold 12,000 copies during its first week of release, less than half the first week sales of The Hip's two previous albums. Another perceived 'low' was accomplished when the album debuted at No. 3 on the Canadian Album chart; normally an outstanding feat if you were anybody but The Hip who had not had album debut at less than No. 2 since *Road Apples*. Even more mortifying to many was that the band would, finally, only sell to gold status certification in Canada, the latest decline in sales popularity on their home turf.

Amazingly the seemingly high point of what was turning into a lackluster release came when *Now for Plan A* crashed the *Billboard* US charts at No. 129 before peaking at No. 44.

In the name of good old-fashioned promotion, The Hip made a series of appearances in several Canadian markets in pop up mini concerts, which included meet and greets and autograph sessions. Some considered the idea a bit cheesy. After all, this was a band with three decades and 12 albums who had opened for The Rolling Stones and The Who.

But for The Hip it was fun and a bit of a gas. They dug it.

Chapter Twenty-Two
Hip On, Hip Off

Following the rush of solo albums and the lightning fast production of *Now for Plan A,* and a predictably long 2013 tour the band entered 2014 in a fairly leisurely state of mind. So much so that The Hip's tour itinerary consisted of only a handful of shows. And while they continued to toy around with new songs, to their way of thinking, they were not in any rush to come out with a new album.

Which did not necessarily mean they weren't above putting a new shine on a very old album.

Fully Completely maintained a lot of sentimental value for the band. It was their third album, one that, production wise, had been a risk and one that had run the gamut from being largely underappreciated to being one of The Hip's true shining moments. It had always been an album that the band members remembered fondly and it could be counted on that songs from that album would make regular appearances on tour.

Fully Completely would turn out to be a worthwhile and wide-ranging look back. The album was totally remastered. It contained two bonus songs,

"Radio Show" and "So Hard Done By," that did not make the cut originally. The album package also contained a 1992 live performance of the album recorded at The Horseshoe Tavern in Toronto. The track "Radio Show" was released as a single to promote the reissue and, to the surprise of many, made a respectable showing on the Canadian Singles chart at No. 29. Getting into the spirit of nostalgia with both feet, The Tragically Hip would perform the *Fully Completely* album in its entirety on several of their 2015 tour stops.

All of which seemed to strike a chord with the band which soon had them actively swapping music and lyrics and making preparation to enter the studio again to record the album entitled *Man Machine Poem*.

With the albums *World Container* and *Now for Plan A*, the band had, perhaps unexpectedly, evolved into a realm of spiritual and existential outlook on life, attitudes and the countless possibilities for a bare bones rock and roll band to do great and mighty things intellectually. And whether they sensed it or not, their sense of mortality may well have started to make an appearance.

The band members may well have sensed that their next album would be like Mercury, an odyssey that would change attitude at the turn of a lyric or the sudden riff. They would need a producer who could deal with emotional peaks and valleys. At the end of the day they found two, Kevin Drew (Broken Social Scene) and Dave Hamelin (The Stills), both quite capable of ramrodding a rock and roll band while showing the sensitivity it would take to make this record the right way. In the fall of 2015, the band repaired to the familiar surroundings of The Bathouse Studio.

Those privy to the *Man Machine Poem* sessions have reported a general ease within the band. Seemingly gone were the pressures of recording an album that would please the masses while satisfying the band's creative soul. The Hip were seemingly channeling their youthful beginnings when stardom was the furthest thing from their mind. The band, musically, was instinctively hitting the right notes and chords and laying the right platform for Downie's lyrics. As noted by producer Drew in a *New York Times* article, Downie's enthusiasm was on display for all to see.

"He would be pacing around the studio, constantly saying 'Let's go as far as we can.' I saw the band write a song in three minutes once. It blew my mind."

Man Machine Poem appeared to be borrowing from its predecessors with the emotional and lyrical themes of the lonely philosopher on an emotional odyssey, contemplating the big and small questions of the universe much in evidence. But whether through circumstance or emotional foreshadowing, there was a sense of impending mortality and contemplating an uncertain future that was appearing in seemingly every song, either front and center or as a sly moment through the lyrics. Make no mistake, the sense of rock and roll was still there but, musically, there were the odd choices that hinted at deeper things.

"In a World Possessed by the Human Mind" is easily a tough-minded entry into the human psyche. Dressed up in a truly haunting, fearful and paranoid journey, the song, accompanied by jangling guitar and sharp interludes, turns a darkly brooding lyrical conversation into a biting commentary on sentimentality and romance. Outside looking inward seems to continue the theme in "What Blue," a simple tale of emotional love done up in subtle deeper shades. Downie's literary influences were much on stage with "Here in the Dark." The song, which highlights a scrap of dialogue from John Steinbeck's *The Grapes of Wrath* is a subtle knock against conflicts that can pull a relationship apart. But if there were secrets just dying to get out, theorists would ultimately point to the song "Tired as Fuck," a Rorschach blot in musical form that digs deep into the issues of physical and mental mortality.

Man Machine Poem would not be released until June 2016 but the tenor and tone of the assembled music was already having those who had heard the finished album expressing some concern. It had always been a safe bet that Downie wore his heart on his sleeve when it came to his lyrics and that, in the case of *Man Machine Poem*, there seemed to be signs of crisis.

The reality of Downie's personal turmoil would begin to seep out, in dribs and drabs of rumor, speculation, reality open to conjecture and the singer's persistence in keeping his private life out of the public eye. What was pointed out in scattered reports from *The Toronto Star* and *The Globe & Mail* was that Downie's father, Edgar, died on October 27, 2015. The day after the funeral Downie was walking with his mother, Lorna, when he suffered a massive seizure. Within days of that episode a notice appeared announcing the sale of his Toronto home. And finally, in literal after the fact reportage consisting, in many cases of a mere sentence, it was reported that Downie and his wife had separated.

Nobody outside of The Tragically Hip's inner circle assumed any of these events were connected. The seizure could have been stress related, resulting from the death of his father. The separation from his wife? Sadly people grow apart. What was known was that Downie had nothing to say about any of it. But his reaction would be typically Downie.

A month after his initial seizure, Downie and *Man Machine Poem* producer Kevin Drew secretly went into a recording studio and Downie wrote and recorded 17 songs in four days. It was an Herculean feat even by Downie's prolific standards. They were also extremely personal songs about people he knew or meant something to him. As the songs, to this date, have never been made public, it appeared that the exercise was more therapeutic. At least, that was the notion that Downie chose to spin in a conversation with *The Globe & Mail.*

"I came home from that recording session thinking that I had reached the peak of the hill," he recalled. "Then two days later, I had this tremendous seizure."

Chapter Twenty-Three
Memory Cues

You could see Downie's scar.

It was not the jagged bunch of mangled, suture-mangled skin. It was not the grotesqueness of a horror film slasher victim or of a ten-car pileup on I-5. In its own way, the head to left temple scar tissue was fairly subtle. Something fairly soft and indented. The result of medical science doing its best to prolong the life of an icon and legend.

And a man.

Always inquisitive and eager to learn new things, Downie became quite familiar with the science and nomenclature of medicine in the immediate aftermath of that December 15 seizure and the discovery that he had a glioblastoma multiforme in his left lobe. In plain English, Downie had brain cancer and the prognosis was not good.

Into the New Year and well into 2016, The Hip front man endured two craniotomies and countless rounds of radiation and chemotherapy. There was vague talk of prolonging his life, with the appropriate statistics trotted out to back that hope up. But it had been made very plain to Downie that what he had was not curable

182

and, in the most candid way possible, that he was on the clock and that the sand was, inexorably, running out.

Downie had been warned that there would be side effects of the procedures. The most telling would be his memory. "It feels like it's all melding together," Downie explained to *The Globe & Mail.* And, as the treatments progressed, he readily acknowledged what was going on in his brain and how his memory lapses were manifesting themselves.

In a conversation with *The National*, he would admit that he was getting real bad with remembering names. As with *The National* interviewer, he had taken to writing names on his hand in some situations, memory cues to jog his mind as to exactly who he was talking to. But even that was an inconsistent process as witness Downie calling *The National* interviewer Doug at one point even while having his actual name, Peter, written on his hand.

An unabashedly inveterate reader before the operations, his ability to comprehend and retain caused an immediate end to that aspect of his life. And he was quite proud of the fact that, midway through the year, he was able to manage 15-20 minutes with a book. But, easily the toughest obstacle to deal with was music and what his faltering memory had done to some of his best musical memories.

He acknowledged to *The Globe & Mail* that conversations about music often suddenly left him out of the loop. In recent conversations he's been known to remember album covers but not the name of the album. The lapses would extend to The Hip's music as well with Downie often struggling to remember favorite songs and even the titles of the bands albums.

But perhaps his most disheartening memory miscues occasionally occurs when Downie claimed in a *National Globe & Mail* interview that he sometimes forgets the names of his children, which brings out some old style Downie humor and then a bit of reflection.

"Will I miss them? I won't know will I? I don't want to die because my youngest son is only ten. I want my kids to be good. I want them to be safe and have a good, long life."

As he passed through the operations and rounds of radiology and chemotherapy, Downie was finding himself limited in his day-to-day life. Rather than band mates, his constant companion was a pillbox that reportedly contains an estimated 50 pills, mostly anti-seizure medication, that must be administered certain times of the day. To that end, Downie's older brother Mike has moved to Toronto and is his constant companion. For Downie, in early 2016, it was just another example of what his life had suddenly and sadly become.

"I can't remember hardly anything," he sighed. "I can't be left alone."

Chapter Twenty-Four
The Last Hurrah

April 2016. Whether or not The Tragically Hip had been informed of Downie's diagnosis is not certain. What is certain is that the band's label sensed, as with previous recent releases, that *Man Machine Poem* would be a challenging record to market. The label was well aware that there had been a steady decline in sales over the past few years and that even another gold album would be cause for concern.

Which is why they were getting an early start. On April 22, nearly two months ahead of the album's release date, the first single "In a World Possessed" was released to mixed but largely positive reviews that accentuated the more daring aspects of the song. As a whole, the normally Canadian radio market would not be overly impressed. The song managed a good but not great No. 22 on the Canadian Alternative chart but did not crack the formal Canadian Singles chart. It would prove to be the highest position as follow up singles "Tired as Fuck" and "What Blue" failed to chart.

In the meantime, behind the scenes The Tragically Hip were wondering how to handle Downie's illness and present it to the public. And what would they do about the expected tour to follow the album's release. Knowing that the news would eventually leak out, the band decided to announce Downie's cancer in a formal press conference on May 25. As it would turn out, going on tour would be a tougher challenge.

The typical Hip show was a strenuous, physically taxing exercise in normal instances. But in Downie's present state there were other issues to consider. The operations and chemotherapy procedures had weakened Downie to the point where it was questioned what kind of performance he was capable of over what could typically turn into a three hour show. Memory issues were another concern. Downie had admitted in *the Globe & Mail* that as recently as six weeks before the start of any proposed tour that he was having trouble remembering the names of The Hip's albums and that forgetting lyrics at a critical point in a show was a real possibility.

Neurologist Dr. James Perry would reiterate that Downie had been cleared to perform and that medical contingencies will be in place to avoid exhaustion and that the singer would be closely monitored.

In a band statement released May 25, the group stated, "After some 30 years together as The Tragically Hip, thousands of shows and hundreds of tours, we've decided to do another one. This feels like the right thing to do for all of us." For his part, Downie would acknowledge several times in the coming weeks that he wanted this tour to be a celebration that would take people away from the sadness.

Those looking for the reported "final tour" to be a lengthy one would be disappointed. The announced tour would be a total of 15 shows between July 22 and August 20. All the shows would be in Canada and would include stops in Victoria, Vancouver, Edmonton, Calgary, Winnipeg, London Toronto, Hamilton, Ontario and, finally, a return to their roots with the last show in Kingston. Other particulars of the tour would be announced along the way. There would be no opening act. And while never completely verified, it was reported that, owing to his memory lapses, Downie would be using a teleprompter.

Suddenly what had been shaping up as just another Hip album and tour had morphed into an unexpected event for the ages. Which meant the band, journalists and, perhaps most importantly, were working overtime to set the record straight with fans. *Man Machine Poem* was written and recorded well before Downie's cancer diagnosis, not after. It is a bit premature to proclaim this as The Hip's final tour and album with the band cautiously saying that, owing to Downie's condition, the band would consider recording and touring again. But at the end of the day, it would all boil down to what the fans felt.

Man Machine Poem was released on June 17, 2016. The album immediately shot to No. 1 on the Canadian Album chart and landed at a rather dreary No. 178 on the US chart. Critics seemingly bent over backwards to be even handed in their assessments but, truth be told, the specter of Downie's disease were never far from their thoughts. Reviews were generally positive with the occasional mediocre or negative review given grudging points for bravery in the wake of the disclosure.

Tickets for the tour almost immediately went on sale with the announcement of the shows and, as it turned out, would cast a pale on the good cheer. Ticket scalpers and resale agencies swooped in and grabbed up all the tickets, which were instantly put up for resale at outlandish prices, well out of reach of The Tragically Hip's most loyal and least well off fans. Fans complained and several news reports chronicling the unfair laws on the books allowing agencies to gouge fans appeared in the media throughout Canada. Eventually the bad vibes made their way back to the band who did their best to alleviate the problem by reconfiguring the shape of their performing stage to free up more seats. Unfortunately, those suddenly additional seats were quickly scooped up as well.

An exasperated Baker addressed the controversy with *The Toronto Sun*. "We're sad and concerned about the situation. We make every effort to make sure it's fair but much is beyond our control. We want fans rather than just the connected."

There was a lot of nervous energy and excitement in The Save-On Foods Arena on July 22, the first stop on the *Man Machine Poem* tour. In the sold out audience, the emotions were running wild as fans screamed out the band's name, reminisced freely about memories of seeing the band for the first time and, yes, broke into spontaneous tears as they dissected Downie and The Hip's future. Backstage it was reportedly all smiles and nervous anticipation. The Tragically Hip were ready to go. It was their time.

Downie came out to thunderous applause, resplendent in his shinny performing finery. The audience responded to his mere presence as a second coming. He was not a savior but, on this night, an argument could be made. The band reared up behind him in a fiery rock and roll blast and The Tragically Hip was off and running. Throughout the two hour, 26-song retrospective of their career, was wired on true passion, giving new life to songs they had not played in years and offering hard and emotion filled renditions of newer material. It was one long party with Downie the ringmaster and whirling dervish, giving no indication that he was a man on borrowed time. In fact, Downie's current life and death struggles were nowhere to be found in the show, with only a quip of "shit happens" tossed off my the singer at one point as even a hint of his real life challenges. At the conclusion of the show, The Tragically Hip stood at center stage, bowing and smiling broadly as they received the accolades. Downie ended the night quite simply when he said "Goodbye. We Love You. Thank you."

The Vancouver shows that followed were a conglomeration of the tour opening show and new sights and sounds. Stories were once again told. People had come from everywhere to experience the band and to share stories of the importance that The Tragically Hip and their music had played out as signposts and cornerstones in their lives. Families spanning several generations hugged and cried. One audience member, old and grey, danced with abandon, rocking out and singing along.

If the band had any rust in the first show, and yes there were some timing issues and missed lyrics which would occasionally surface throughout the tour and which would be smoothed over with the help of strategically placed teleprompters, they were quickly forgotten and chalked up to being part of the experience. The band knew their place in Vancouver, flexing considerable muscle throughout the 30-song set as the perfect backdrop for Downie's manic/passionate performance. And on those occasions when Downie seemed to temporarily lose his way, they were quick to blast out an impromptu bridge or solo to allow Downie to catch his mental breath.

"It smells like dope in here," the singer yelled early in the show, escaping into the vibe and the crowd. "It's almost unsettling."

As each of the Vancouver shows concluded, the band took their expected group bow. Then the band left the stage, leaving Downie alone to soak up the adulation. "Thank you. Thank you. It means a lot."

The band was so intent on making what might well be their last tour that they did want any outside distractions getting in the way. Especially when it came to the media. Consequently, the band did no interviews and had very little photo access during the tour. Some in the press complained but not really that hard. They kind of understood the sanctity and purity that had developed in the band's world at this moment. And even if they didn't, The Hip could care less. They were working real hard to make this tour perfect and they were not going to let prying eyes get in the way.

The Hip appeared to be hitting their stride during their Edmonton shows. The band provided some truly masterful rock moments in the two-hour plus show and worked real hard at making what could be the last time a truly magic night. Downie, during the first of the shows, seemed keenly aware and, reportedly, cognizant of how his mortality was playing into the show. When not belting out manic and heartfelt lyrics while owning the stage in an electric/dramatic way, Downie would acknowledge the songs with reverence and good cheer. He had been emotionally on fire all through the tour but when it came time to call it a night, there seemed to be an extra edge and no small amount of tears.

"Walk to the horizon! Thank you from the bottom of our hearts. Thank you ladies and gentlemen. Behold! The end! The motorcycle gang member! The son of the chameleon! We've had a wonderful night here tonight and every night. Love you."

Winnipeg brought back some ironic memories. Early in The Hip's career, the group had a tough time catching on in that neck of the woods and, as Downie reminded the sold out audience that night, they had been fired at least half a dozen times. But when the crowd responded to that bit of history in a boisterous, negative manner, the singer played peacemaker when he said, "its okay. It's time to forgive and forget."

Significant in the tour had been The Hip's insistence on changing up the set list literally every show. Those hoping for an all the hits and favorite album cuts were often met with obscurities and whole albums being excluded from the concert. The Winnipeg show would be no exception and led to one frustrated member of the audience to tweet worst set list ever. But those isolated complaints were more than compensated by the pure majesty, good time rock and roll vibe and no small amount of humility coming from the band.

The London show was typified by never ending good cheer. People meeting old and new friends amid Hip tales of first times and long distance travels to see the band. Obviously the band was the main attraction but the real life energy made for a more than admirable supporting cast. There was also an unbridled urgency as each song unfolded. This could very well be the last time the band appeared live and people were determined to enjoy and embrace every second of it.

The Toronto shows appeared to reach a creative apex. Good times, good music were the order of the day. And it was not just for the fans. Beginning with the first show, there seemed solidarity, an unspoken comradery in the way they stood close together and played their parts. It was a sign that more than 30 years together had forged a closeness that could not be broken apart. To this point in the tour, the notion of Downie being terminally ill had seemed to vanish from the equation.

But there was a moment during the first show that indicated that reality was still uppermost in their minds. Downie had just completed a manic bit of business and the band was about to launch into a monster jam. But it appeared that Downie wasn't finished as he danced over to where Baker was playing and continued to gyrate and scream out some scat vocals. Suddenly Baker reached out and tapped Baker on the shoulder. As it would turn out, it was a signal employed when Downie seemed to forget that part of his regimen was to take intermittent breaks during the show to keep his energy up. Downie got the picture and went off stage as the band continued to rock.

Downie was definitely energized during the second Toronto show. At one point early in the show during a frantic bit of song and dance, he admonished the crowd to get politically and socially active, especially as it pertained to Canadian First Nation rights. "Let's get some fucking courage!" he railed.

Moments later he would bring down the house when he pretended to urinate on drummer Fay's kit.

The show was a musical and emotional rite of passage as hugs, kisses, memories and tears formed a literal rainbow over the stage and the band as The Hip continued the tour policy of playing their hearts out. Like previous nights, the show ended with Downie on the stage, soaking up the adulation and taking his bows. His final words this night were cryptic but no less touching.

"And it just disappears. It just disappears. And that's okay too."

By the time The Hip got to Hamilton, one began to wonder if it was the same group of diehard fans that had been following the band from show to show. The emotions and memories seemed the same, as did the laughs and cries. The show was long and inclusive of just about every album in the band's catalogue. The performance was alternately joyous and poignant. The notion that this could, indeed, be the last Hip tour was very much in the thoughts of the band and those in the sold out arena. These would be thoughts that were very much in the air when Downie stood alone at the end of the show.

"It was a lot of fun," he told the cheering crowd. "That is the main idea. None of it will last much longer than the particular phone you're shooting it on. And that's okay. It will be the little feelings that will pop up here and there."

Even before the *Man Machine Poem* tour started, the vibe was definitely on the August 20 final show in Kingston. The notion of The Tragically Hip literally and spiritually bringing it all full circle to where the band began reeked of the best possible nostalgia. Sure, on a certain level, it seemed so corny and, perhaps, a bit cheesy. But, at the end of the day, it was just so damned right and appropriate and had captured the hopes, dreams, support and dedication from the town that just could not be denied. With the show long since sold out and millions across the country hoping for either another or first chance at seeing the band, the fairy godmother of Hipdom strategically appeared.

The Canadian Broadcasting Corporation (CBC), the prime broadcaster of television and radio content in the country, stepped in with an offer to good to resist. The CBC would simulcast, commercial free The Tragically Hip's Kingston concert to all of its major television and radio outlets under the title The Tragically Hip: A National Celebration. Subsequently several live stream viewings, including one in Kingston's Market Square. The city of Kingston finally made the band's homecoming official when it voted to declare the day of the concert Tragically Hip Day. A reported 11.7 million people would take advantage of the CBC's generosity.

Crowds began gathering outside the concert hall hours before the show was scheduled to start. Those with the prized tickets mixed and mingled joyously and with a large dose of sentiment in and around the city proper, talking in highly personal and often tearful terms of how their lives had intersected with the band's over the years and what the impact of a Canadian band carrying the banner for their country meant to them. Among them was the Canadian Prime Minister Justin Trudeau who had been a fan of The Hip since high school and, over the years, had formed a strong bond with the band.

For Trudeau, protocol and influence went out the window on that day. He walked the streets of Kingston in a joyous daze, celebrating with fans and being beseeched by media for his feelings on the day and the band. His responses were true and heartfelt. The man who ran the country was a fan for the day.

In difference to the growing crowds, the doors opened two hours early and those with tickets walked happily through, alternately delighted and subdued at what they were about to see and hear. Backstage the band, reportedly, was reflecting similar thoughts, making small talk and welcoming well- wishers with hugs, smiling and laughing a nervous laughter. And, most certainly, acknowledging, inwardly, that the time had certainly come and that Kingston might really be there last hurrah.

A stirring rendition of "O' Canada," sung by thousands of fans, welcomed the band to the stage. Then it was on to the last hurrah, a two-hour plus, nearly 30 songs that, collectively, had meant so much to so many. One did not have to stretch to realize that The Hip were trying extra hard for the hometown folks. The band kicked each tune into overdrive with monstrous riffs and runs just that little bit extra that translated into so much more. Downie was on fire throughout. His interpretation of songs he had sung countless times were reaching that much higher, wringing every possible bit of emotion, drama and sentimentality of them. His demeanor on stage was loose but no less passionate. Downie knew the score. He wasn't going to give what could be his last shot anything but everything he could muster.

Downie stood center stage, alone for what may

well have been the final time. There were tears in his eyes. "Thank you for a great tour and a great show. I enjoyed the hell out of it. Thank you for keeping me pushing. Thank you for listening everybody. Thank you for listening period...

...Have a nice life."

Chapter Twenty-Five
Rio: What Hip Means

The world stopped on the last night of The Tragically Hip's final show of their Man, Machine Poem tour in Kingston.

The day had long since been declared a national holiday. Streets were blocked. Kingston, on most nights, could be a swinging place if you asked the locals. But this was Saturday night and even the hot spots in Kingston had either shut down all together or were putting in only minimal effort to compete with that night's main attraction. It was a Saturday night but, for all intents and purposes, the entire country of Canada had stopped, their minds and emotions centered in rapt attention on a band literally everyone in Canada had grown up with.

People were lining the streets of Kingston. The 7000 available seats for the final concert had been immediately snapped up but outside there was literally standing room only. Aerial shots from local media outlets found a crowd of thousands snaking out from the concert hall and filling every possible nook of space on the streets. The crowd spanned generations. Some were elder-statesmen, families with offspring of various ages scurried around excitedly. This was a scene indicative of people who had been around The Tragically Hip all their days, or at least the important ones.

For those outside, it was bliss rather than disappointment at not being part of the sold-out show. It was nirvana, people reconnecting with old friends or glad handing strangers as if they were long lost brothers and sisters, sharing memories, happy and sad, of the band and the important moments in their lives that were personified by The Hip's music. It was a joyous moment caught in time.

And it was a joy being shared by Canadians thousands of miles away in Rio de Janeiro. The Canadian Olympic team had just concluded their best Olympic games in years and were in a spirit to celebrate and party. And they were about to be rewarded due to the seemingly unending generosity of the CBC.

Already considered Canada's Santa for simulcasting The Tragically Hip's final show on simulcast to an estimated 11.7 million people all across the provinces, the media giant added frosting to the cake when it cut away from its nonstop coverage of the Olympics to televise The Hip concert for the Canadians in Rio. The Canadian Consulate organized a Tragically Hip concert watching party while spur of the moment gatherings popped up all across the Olympic village. And it would be gatherings that would mirror what was going on in Kingston.

To athletes from other countries who happened to wander in on the Hip experience, it must have seemed like being dropped into the middle of an alien world.

With rare exception of pockets of support in the US, nobody truly had a clue as to what The Tragically Hip were all about. But once the band hit the stage and the first rocking guitar chords were unleashed, music as a universal language could suddenly add 'international' to its description.

As the band's images flickered across Rio screens, there were good-natured shouts from the Canadian athletes to turn the sound up. In front of the large screens, athletes, many dressed in their Olympic uniforms and wearing their newly won medals, danced wildly. It seemed like everybody had met a member of the band at one time or another and all had stories to tell. Some had met at a Hip concert, many had fallen in love with the sounds of the band playing in the background. All were saddened at the news of Downie's illness and already waxing nostalgic at the prospect of The Tragically Hip fading away, except in their memories.

On the night of The Tragically Hip's last show, this is what it meant to loyal and loving fans, miles and miles apart. But it also meant so much more. The cross world involvement of that final concert also effectively encapsulated what it means to be a symbol of nationalism at its finest.

The Tragically Hip, as witness the estimated 12 million people who joined the Olympians who tuned in for the band's possible last hurrah, was testament to the power of a group to, musically and otherwise, personify the hopes and dreams of an entire nation. It happens occasionally in the non-entertainment world, as witnessed with the election of President Barack Obama in the mid 2000's. But when it comes to music, it's often all too fly-by-night and of-the-moment for many to form a tight bond of emotional attachment. A case has often been made that Bruce Springsteen, The Rolling Stones and David Bowie were truly musicians of the masses but, on this night, nobody, either in Canada or in Rio, could argue that when it came to representing the human condition, The Hip were truly hip.

But in saying goodbye for, perhaps, the final time, The Tragically Hip, the personification of 'one of us,' had arrived as a true band of the people. They were small town boys who used their passion to make it out, something we all aspire to even in our dreams. They were talented in the extreme but went about their business in a subtle, below the radar, scandal free manner. Perhaps most importantly, they were able to walk among us, friendly, honest and ultimately real and true to their convictions.

Twelve million people don't follow the every twist and turn of a 30-year career because the band is the flavor of the moment. They don't take three hours out of a time of celebrating their own glories to watch just any band. They do it out of a sincere belief and adoration.

For fans of The Tragically Hip, that night in Canada and in Rio, it all boiled down to truth...

...And love.

Chapter Twenty-Six
Gone Fishing, Now What?

The Hip were in a state of exultation as the band walked off the stage in Kingston. They were also in a state of mental and emotional exhaustion. What they craved was to quite simply get away from it all. And what that meant way to go way north and do some fishing along the James Bay Coast.

The band and particularly Downie found themselves at peace in the soothing surroundings as they fished and explored the area while being guided by members of the indigenous tribes. And, according to stories by *The Toronto Star, CBC News.com* and *Global News.com* among others, Downie, who had been making pro First Nation Rights throughout the just concluded tour, felt spiritually entwined with the people and their struggles during these period and was ultimately encouraged to step forward publically on their behalf whenever possible.

Eventually the band's time in relative paradise ended and they returned to the real world where they were constantly under scrutiny by the media and fans alike. There were the constant inquiries about Downie's health. There were also persistent rumors about future albums, tours and how long the band would officially be together. The Hip remained silent on just about every count, refusing to do interviews over the coming months.

But when pressed, or if they were of a mind, band members would occasionally drop hints as to what the future might bring. In response to a fan tweet, as reported by *The Kingston Whip Standard*, Baker tweeted out "We never said anything about this being the end. There is more to come." But Baker's tweet contained nothing more.

Likewise, Downie, in a *Globe & Mail* feature, matter of factly acknowledged that the band had been working on some things since the end of the tour but would not be specific. Which did not necessarily mean that The Hip were not busy. Point of fact, Downie's growing interest in Indian rights would soon put him in the spotlight.

Downie's brother, Mike, came to him with a story he had discovered from a CBC radio documentary about a young Indian boy named Chanie Wenjack who, in 1966, escaped from an Indian residential school and, subsequently died of exposure while attempting to walk the 400 miles to his home. It was a sad tale but Downie immediately saw it as something much deeper and in line with his long held advocacy for Indian rights in Canada.

"Chanie haunts me," he disclosed in a written essay on the *Secret Path* website. "His story is Canada's story. This is about Canada. We are not the country we thought we were. We are all accountable."

Including Downie who immediately took it upon himself to help bring Chanie's plight and that of all of

Canada's indigenous population to the masses. He would soon discover that he was not alone in wanting to help. Famed graphic novelist Jeff Lemire created a graphic novel of the Chanie story which would ultimately be made into an animated feature. For his part, Downie and the *Man Machine Poem* producers Kevin Drew and Dave Hamelin, along with musicians Charles Spearin, Ohad Benchetrit, Kevin Hearn and Dave Koster created a series of songs, written and sung by Downie that told the story of Chanie in an emotional, heartfelt manner that would finally force people to face the consequences of turning their backs on an important issue.

"You start looking at all this stuff," said Downie on the Secret Path website, "and it does start putting a damper on all the stuff we're doing to celebrate 150 years of nationhood."

The album, entitled *The Secret Path*, whose proceeds would go to a fund dedicated to Chantie's memory and to supporting First Person Rights (which would ultimately gather more than $3 million in donations), would be a wild success, peaking at No. 4 on the Canadian Album chart and, when combined with the exposure offered by the graphic novel and the animated film, would go a long way toward doing right by Canada's Indian population.

Downie, continuing to deal with the impact of his cancer and occasional bouts of guilt over how good a father he had been, would ultimately look at what he had done with *The Secret Path* as a bright spot in his life, one that might well be an important part of any legacy he might well have.

"If this is the last thing I do, then I'm happy."

Epilogue
If This Be the End

More than three decades, 15 albums, hundreds of tours and thousands of shows. If this is the end of the road, then it's been one hell of a ride. If it is truly the end.

Reality comes in many shapes, sizes and situations. Nothing is absolute, especially in the world of rock and roll. If the Man, Machine Poem tour, with all its celebratory, sad and joyous moments, is truly the last dance for The Tragically Hip, then so be it. We can only hope that the band goes quietly and gently into the good night.

But there just might be a next chapter in The Tragically Hip saga to consider.

The prognosis for Downie is incurable but not necessarily a death sentence. Doctors have said that patients with his particular brand of cancer have been known to survive years after the diagnosis and, by association, have been fairly productive. And it's a sure bet that Baker, Fay, Sinclair and Langlois, being the pure musicians that they are, will be heard from in the form of solo albums, side projects and producing.

But as to The Hip proper? It's a safe bet that the band will be operative to the extent that Downie's condition holds or deteriorates. There maybe an occasional album of new material. The Hip may tour again under the right circumstances, albeit on a much shorter schedule.

Bottom line: What Is Hip has been the whole story of a band that a lot of people did not know even existed while, at the same time, they were the darlings of millions of fans who have lived and breathed their brand of rock and roll with soul and an eye constantly on the prize which was something deeper and personal.

If there is truly a God in rock and roll heaven, The Tragically Hip will live forever.

APPENDIX

AWARDS AND HONORS

SOCIETY OF COMPOSERS, AUTHORS AND
MUSIC PUBLISHERS OF CANADA
1997: National Achievement Award

CANADA'S WALK OF FAME
2002: Inducted in Toronto.

CANADA'S MUSIC HALL OF FAME
2005: Inducted at the Juno Awards in Winnipeg.

ROYAL CONSERVATORY OF MUSIC
2006: Presented with an Honorary Fellowship in
Toronto.

GOVERNOR GENERAL'S PERFORMING ARTS
AWARDS
2008: Presented the National Arts Center Award in
Ottawa.

JUNO AWARDS
1990: Most Promising Group of the Year
1991: Canadian Entertainer of the Year
1993; Canadian Entertainer of the Year
1995: Group of the Year
1997: Group of the Year
1997: Album of the Year (*Trouble at the Henouse*)

1997: North Star Rock Album of the Year
(*Trouble at the Henhouse*)

1999: Best Rock Album (*Phantom Power*)

1999: Best Album Design (*Phantom Power*)

2000: Best Single (*Bobcaygeon*)

2001: Best Rock Album (*Music@Work*)

2006: CD/DVD Artwork Design of the Year
(*Hipeponymous*)

2006: Music DVD of the Year (*Hipeponymous*)

SOUNDTRACK CONTRIBUTIONS

1993: *A Man in Uniform* (movie) Songs: "Radio Show," "Pigeon Camera"

1995: *Due South* (television) Song: "At the Hundredth Meridian"

1996: *Kids In the Hall: Brain Candy* (movie) Song: "Butts Wigglin"

1996: *The Boys Club* (movie) Song: "Coconut Crème"

1996: *Bonjour Timothy* (movie) Songs: "Three Pistols", "Bring It All Back"

1997: *The Sweet Hereafter* (movie) Song: "Courage"

2002: *Men with Brooms* (movie) Songs: "Silver Road," "Throwing Off Glass," "Oh Honey," "Poets"

2006: *Comeback Season* (movie) Song: "Vaccination Scar"

2006: *Trailer Park Boys: The Movie* (movie) Songs: "Bobcaygeon," "38 Years Old," "Scared"

2008: *Jumper* (movie) Song: "Ahead by a Century"

2009: *Rise Up: Canadian Pop Music In The 1980's* (television movie documentary) Song: "New Orleans is Sinking"

2009: *Flashpoint* (television) Song: "Now the Struggle Has A Name" (uncredited)

2010: *Being Erica* (television) Song: "Fifty Mission Cap"

2014: *Devil's Mile* (movie) Song: "Locked in the Trunk of a Car"

SOURCES

INTERVIEWS
I would like to thank Kenny Sprackman and Hugh Segal for their time and insights. Also thanks to the mystery contributor who exchanged pages of obscurities for his anonymity. Nobody will ever know.

BOOKS
Have Not Been the Same: The CanRock Renaissance by Michael Barclay and Jason Schneider (ECW Press)

WEBSITES
CBC News.com, CBC Music.com, TragicallyHip.com, TSN.com, KickassCanadians.com, ReverrendGuitars.com, Canoe.com, Prezi.com, The Whig.com, EarOfNewt.com, Nicholas Jennings.com, Jam Canoe.com, Geocities.com, BBC News.com, TheHip.com, Hipfans.com, HipOnline.com, GordDownie.com, Guitar.com, Jam.com, Live Daily.com, Artist Trove.com, CTV.com, Popmatters.com

NEWSPAPERS
The Kingston Whig Standard, The Globe & Mail, Queens University Journal, Ottawa Citizen, The North Bay Nugget, The Georgia Straight, The London Free Press, Winnipeg Free Press, The Chicago Tribune, The Windsor Star, The Hamilton Spectator, Tucson Weekly, The Toledo Blade, The Rochester City

Newspaper, The Toronto Sun, The Buffalo News, Niagara Falls Review, The Post Standard, New York Times, The National.com.

MAGAZINES
Billboard, Toro, Maclean's, Canadian Musician, Drop D, No Depression,

MISCELLANEOUS
Joe Pater blog, The Tragically Hip Unreleased Information Page, QCBC podcast, Secret Path website, University of Saskatchewan Master's Thesis by Paul David Aikenhead entitled *Man Sized Inside: The History of The Construction of Masculinity in the Tragically Hip's Album Fully Completed.*

About the Author

New York Times bestselling author Marc Shapiro has written more than 60 nonfiction celebrity biographies, more than two-dozen comic books, numerous short stories and poetry, and three short form screenplays. He is also a veteran freelance entertainment journalist.

His young adult book *JK Rowling: The Wizard Behind Harry Potter* was on *The New York Times* bestseller list for four straight weeks. His fact-based book *Total Titanic* was also on *The Los Angeles Times* bestseller list for four weeks. *Justin Bieber: The Fever* was on the nationwide Canadian bestseller list for several weeks.

Shapiro has written books on such personalities as Shonda Rhimes, George Harrison, Carlos Santana, Annette Funicello, Lorde, Lindsay Johan, E.L. James, Jamie Dornan, Dakota Johnson, Adele and countless others. He also co-authored the autobiography of mixed martial arts fighter Tito Ortiz, *This Is Gonna Hurt: The Life of a Mixed Martial Arts Champion*.

He is currently working on a biography of Mary Tyler Moore as well as updating his biographies of Gillian Anderson and Lucy Lawless for Riverdale Avenue Books.

Other Riverdale Avenue Books Titles by Marc Shapiro

Hey Joe: The Unauthorized Biography of a Rock Classic

Trump This! The Life and Times of Donald Trump, An Unauthorized Biography

The Secret Life of EL James

The Real Steele: The Unauthorized Biography of Dakota Johnson

Inside Grey's Anatomy: The Unauthorized Biography of Jamie Dornan

Annette Funicello: America's Sweetheart

Game: The Resurrection of Tim Tebow

Legally Bieber: Justin Bieber at 18

Lindsay Lohan: Fully Loaded, From Disney to Disaster

Lorde: Your Heroine, How This Young Feminist Broke the Rules and Succeeded

We Love Jenni: An Unauthorized Biography

Who Is Katie Holmes? An Unauthorized Biography

*Norman Reedus: True Tales of The Waking Dead's
Zombie Hunter, An Unauthorized Biography*

*Welcome to Shondaland: An Unauthorized Biography
of Shonda Rhimes*

46725412R00125

Made in the USA
Middletown, DE
07 August 2017